PR

A Mission Without Borders

"I am alive today thanks to the bravery and faith of Chad—and this book shows the behind-the-scenes of my own rescue. Again and again Chad risks his own life to save others from the frontlines. The world is a better place because of him."

—BENJAMIN HALL, FOX NEWS CORRESPONDENT AND *NEW YORK TIMES* BESTSELLING AUTHOR OF *SAVED*

"Chad and his team seem to perform best when bullets are flying, artillery is exploding, and people need his help. *A Mission Without Borders* is packed with riveting stories of harrowing rescues and aid missions in war-torn Ukraine, all with the help of the Lord. Needless to say, it's a must read."

—SHAWN RYAN, FORMER US NAVY SEAL AND CIA CONTRACTOR, AND HOST OF THE *SHAWN RYAN SHOW*

"Chad's life embodies the values of courage, humility, and faith. His unparalleled bravery and love have displayed a willingness to live out Jesus' words in John 15:13: 'Greater love has no one than this: to lay down one's life for one's friends.' These stories are remarkable human feats, and yet Chad returns the glory to Him."

—KAYLEIGH MCENANY, FORMER WHITE HOUSE PRESS SECRETARY AND COHOST OF *OUTNUMBERED*, FOX NEWS

"The World War II United States Marines were known as the Old Breed. Well, this is a story written by the New Breed of USMC veterans, who have personally experienced the harrowing rescues and missions in war-torn Ukraine. This is an uplifting story reminding us of our humanity and the Lord's love for all people in all nations."

—SECRETARY CHRISTOPHER MILLER, FORMER US SECRETARY OF DEFENSE AND US ARMY SPECIAL FORCES (COL RETIRED)

"*A Mission Without Borders* is a powerful reminder that people are more important than borders or politics. In this intense, true story Chad and his team show us what dramatic heroism and selfless sacrifice really are. Chad is a modern-day international hero, and I'm proud to call him a friend."

—ERIC METAXAS, #1 *NEW YORK TIMES* BESTSELLING AUTHOR
AND HOST OF *THE ERIC METAXAS RADIO SHOW*

"Nothing makes a story more intriguing than knowing that the teller has 'been there and done that.' If Chad's stories don't move you so much that you can't stop reading, grab your wrist and check for a pulse."

—SEAN PATRICK FLANERY, AWARD-WINNING ACTOR IN *BOONDOCK SAINTS, POWDER, YOUNG INDIANA JONES*, AND MORE

"Chad Robichaux, a fellow Marine, is an example of unwavering faith in God and a testament to the strength He provides us during the most difficult situations. This story showcases elite operators who place their trust in God, answer His calling, and change the trajectory of their own lives and, more importantly, the lives of others."

—MARK "OZ" GEIST, BESTSELLING COAUTHOR OF *13 HOURS*, US MARINE CORPS VETERAN, AND MEMBER OF THE BENGHAZI ANNEX SECURITY TEAM

"This book will move and inspire you, and I recommend it with the highest conviction! I am so thankful that God called upon the Robichaux family to display the love of Jesus and the courage his Spirit provides to bring healing and hope."

—JASE ROBERTSON, STAR OF *DUCK DYNASTY* AND *DUCK FAMILY TREASURE*

"I was deeply moved and profoundly motivated by Chad Robichaux's latest book *A Mission Without Borders*. The gripping story of heroism and selfless service in battle-torn Ukraine exposes both the worst and the best of humanity, reveals concrete truths about sonship and fatherhood, and draws the reader's heart much closer to our own Father and Creator. It also reveals the incredible service Mighty Oaks Foundation provides to those fighting for freedom in America and abroad. It is a *must read*."

—TOMMY WALLER, FORMER COMMANDER OF USMC 3D FORCE RECONNAISSANCE COMPANY (LTCOL RETIRED) AND PRESIDENT AND CEO OF CENTER FOR SECURITY POLICY

"In a day and age where we are beat down with negativity, sensationalism, and constant bad news, every now and then comes a story that shines like a light in the darkness. *A Mission Without Borders* is that story. It is about doing good in the midst of bad and chaos. If you are tired of the darkness and need a little light, read this book."

—Jason Redman, US Navy SEAL (LT retired) and *New York Times* bestselling author of *The Trident* and *Overcome*

"Some men run away from trouble, and some run toward trouble to help those suffering. Chad Robichaux is one of those unique people who does difficult things to help those who cannot help themselves. *A Mission Without Borders* is an encouraging, hope-filled commentary on the war in Ukraine. Beyond political jargon and posturing, it gives the reader an open window into current events and offers a response of faith."

—Allen Jackson, senior pastor of World Outreach Church, host of *Culture & Christianity*, and author of *Big Trouble Ahead*

"As someone who has witnessed the brutal realities of the frontlines, I know the human cost of service and answering the call to help our fellow man. In *A Mission Without Borders* Chad's unwavering commitment to that call is on full display. At a time where our world is plagued by wars on multiple fronts, we need more brave individuals like him who are ready to make a positive difference in the world."

—Tyler Merritt, CEO of Nine Line Apparel and US Army Special Operations CDR (CPT retired)

"Chad is part of our church family and made ten trips to Ukraine in the months after the war started. This book helps the American reader understand what the war is like in Ukraine for everyday people and the extreme dangers and suffering they have faced. At the same time, it is the story of a father trusting God for his son, moving from fear to faith."

—Jeff Wells, senior pastor of WoodsEdge Community Church and author of *Unhurried Time with God*

"*A Mission Without Borders* is a testament to the resilience of the human spirit and the power of courage and compassion in action. Chad's unwavering commitment to brave service, along with his courage to embark on a journey filled with uncertainty, is nothing short of inspiring."

—CHAD PRATHER, HOST OF *THE CHAD PRATHER SHOW*

"Chad demonstrates the power and importance of fatherhood, both in the flesh with our earthly fathers and in the spirit with our heavenly Father. As Chad and his son navigate the dangerous front lines of the Russian–Ukrainian invasion, their unwavering dedication to serving others in need highlights their strength, courage, and commitment to God and people."

—JACK BREWER, US COMMISSIONER AND FORMER NFL STAR

"So many lies and so much disinformation swirl around the brutal war in Ukraine. *A Mission Without Borders* tells the gripping truth of what is actually happening. Chad and his son's story demonstrates the transformative power of faith and resilience in the face of adversity. Read it and be inspired."

—SEBASTIAN GORKA, PhD, FORMER STRATEGIST TO PRESIDENT TRUMP
AND AUTHOR OF THE *NEW YORK TIMES* BESTSELLER *DEFEATING JIHAD*

"Chad and his team remind me of one of my favorite quotes: 'The only necessary for the triumph of evil is for good men to do nothing.' *A Mission Without Borders* is a story of God opening doors for unordinary men who are unafraid to do extraordinary things."

ADAM LAROCHE, FORMER MAJOR LEAGUE BASEBALL STAR
AND FOUNDER OF THE E3 RANCH FOUNDATION

A MISSION
WITHOUT BORDERS

WHY A FATHER AND SON RISKED
IT ALL FOR THE PEOPLE OF UKRAINE

Chad Robichaux

with CRAIG BORLASE

NELSON
BOOKS

An Imprint of Thomas Nelson

Published in Nashville, Tennessee, by Nelson Books, an imprint of Thomas Nelson. Nelson Books and Thomas Nelson are registered trademarks of HarperCollins Christian Publishing, Inc.

Published in association with The Howard Literary Agency, 102 Yellowood Drive, West Monroe, LA 71291. Represented by John Howard.

Thomas Nelson titles may be purchased in bulk for educational, business, fundraising, or sales promotional use. For information, please email SpecialMarkets@ThomasNelson.com.

ISBN 978-1-4002-5080-6 (ITPE)

Library of Congress Cataloging-in-Publication Data

Names: Robichaux, Chad, 1975- author.
Title: A mission without borders : why a father and son risked it all for the people of Ukraine / Chad Robichaux.
Other titles: Why a father and son risked it all for the people of Ukraine
Description: Nashville, Tennessee : Thomas Nelson, [2024] | Summary: "Author, speaker, and former Force Recon Marine Chad Robichaux offers an honest, no-holds-barred account of what has really been happening in Ukraine and shares powerful stories that are soaked in resiliency and determination, faith and sacrifice in the face of overwhelming opposition"-- Provided by publisher.
Identifiers: LCCN 2024000501 (print) | LCCN 2024000502 (ebook) | ISBN 9781400247752 (hardcover) | ISBN 9781400247844 (ebook)
Subjects: LCSH: Russian Invasion of Ukraine, 2022---Personal narratives, American. | Robichaux, Chad, 1975- | Russian Invasion of Ukraine, 2022---Participation, Foreign. | Russian Invasion of Ukraine, 2022---Refugees. | Humanitarian assistance--Ukraine. | Volunteer workers in search and rescue operations--Ukraine--Biography. | Mighty Oaks Foundation. | Robichaux, Hunter.
Classification: LCC DK5501.U6 R63 2024 (print) | LCC DK5501.U6 (ebook) | DDC 947.7086--dc23/eng/20240223
LC record available at https://lccn.loc.gov/2024000501
LC ebook record available at https://lccn.loc.gov/2024000502

This book is dedicated to all whose hearts ache with a burden for others in need and to those with the courage to put politics, populist opinions, and borders aside and take action for the sake of doing what is right.

To all the people of Ukraine, who did not ask for a political war over ideology, land, greed, and corruption and simply desire to live free—we see you, we stand with you, and we pray for God to bring peace to your lives and land.

CONTENTS

FOREWORD

I first crossed paths with Chad Robichaux in 2021 shortly after the fall of Kabul to the Taliban. President Biden had ordered the disastrous, full withdrawal of US military forces, creating chaos and leaving many Afghans to desperately search for a way out. I was in Qatar with the organization I help lead, Samaritan's Purse, to see how we could help the Afghans who had made it out but left everything behind. I soon learned that Chad was leading a small group of brave civilians who rushed into the danger to rescue thousands of innocent Afghans desperate to escape. Without Chad and his team, many of those individuals and their families likely would have been killed for their assistance to the US military prior to the withdrawal.

As a former Army Ranger, I had served multiple combat deployments in Afghanistan and knew how valuable the work of Afghan civilians had been to our mission there. I called many of them my friends. I was thankful and proud of the work Chad was doing, and Samaritan's Purse committed to helping him with this critical effort to save lives.

A few years later, as Samaritan's Purse began providing emergency relief immediately after the invasion of Ukraine, I learned that Chad was continuing his lifesaving rescue missions there. This time he was traveling to the front lines, bringing vulnerable people to safety and partnering with local community groups, including churches, to supply needed assistance to those who chose to stay.

Once again I applauded his efforts. However, it wasn't until I read *A Mission Without Borders* that I understood the extent of his service and sacrifice. The book is a gripping account of Chad's determination to help the people of Ukraine, not only risking his own life but living under constant fear for the safety of his son Hunter. As the father of four children myself, I can't imagine the strain of hearing explosions as the background noise to your son's voice on the phone. It was an encouragement to read how this father and son, both former Marines, drew closer together to overcome the mental, emotional, and physical challenges of their mission.

One of the things that has always impressed me about Chad is that he doesn't just talk about how he would like to help others; he acts. Many people wonder what their calling is and sit on their hands while saying that they are waiting for a sign from God. When I think of Chad, I'm reminded of the story of the disciples in the storm-tossed boat found in Scripture (Matthew 14:22–33). Although Peter was terrified like the others, he eventually stepped out of the boat and found that he could walk on the water. Instead of being complacent by sitting in the boat, he didn't let his doubt and fear keep him from action. He walked toward Jesus and trusted Him to guide his steps. If you want to be a part of a miracle, then you have to get out of the boat. That's what Chad does, and God has blessed him for it.

Even more important and inspirational, however, is the testimony of God's faithfulness contained in these pages. Chad outlines in sometimes-painful detail how the Lord revived his own faith. At its heart, *A Mission Without Borders* is a Gospel story—a father and son who find ultimate peace as they surrender to their heavenly Father through a relationship with His son, Jesus Christ. The Bible tells us, "For God so loved the world that he gave his one and only Son, that whoever believes in him shall not perish but have eternal life" (John 3:16). This is the message that is woven throughout these pages in the midst of the compelling stories of danger and selfless service.

I pray that as you read this book, you will see a clear vision of God's eternal truth, and that it will draw you closer to the Lord. If you have never repented of your sins and accepted Jesus as Lord of your life, I hope that He uses this story to invite you into an eternal relationship with your heavenly Father, who loves you and wants to bring you peace in the midst of any circumstance. All it takes is a simple prayer to acknowledge

Jesus as Savior and ask Him to forgive your sins. Then, like Chad and Hunter, you can rest in the knowledge that "to all who did receive him, to those who believed in his name, he gave the right to become children of God" (John 1:12).

Edward Graham
Chief Operating Officer
Samaritan's Purse International Relief

AUTHOR'S NOTE

This book is not an attempt to cover the geopolitics of the Russia–Ukraine war. *A Mission Without Borders* is the story of me, my son, and the brave individuals we partnered with. We were in Ukraine to help innocent people who were victims of this war and unable to help themselves, and along the way I learned so much about myself, my son, and the providential hand of God. I went from fear to faith, and I hope these lessons will encourage you in the fears you may face in your everyday lives. But while the story I'm telling in this book is faith-filled and deeply personal, we can't ignore the politics. So before you dive in, I think it's important that I briefly share my position on this unnecessary, unfortunate, and brutal war taking place in Ukraine.

Ever since February 2022 I've received continuous media requests to talk about the Russian invasion of Ukraine. Networks like Fox News, Newsmax, The Blaze, and several larger podcasts have all wanted to hear about the work we were engaged in there. And at some point in the interviews they've all asked a version of the same simple question: Why would I choose to get involved in a war tainted by so much corruption?

It's not just journalists who've been wondering. I've received messages from donors and people on social media who are upset about the billions in US taxpayer dollars given to President Zelensky with little to no Congressional oversight.

I get it. In fact I agree with most of the points that people have raised. I've been on the front lines in Ukraine, and I've not seen much evidence that those billions of dollars given by the US have been spent on equipment. Almost every Ukrainian unit I've visited has been undersupplied. I've spent the last year raising money for the simplest of necessary items a soldier would need, such as torniquets and basic medical supplies, and risking both my life and my team's lives to deliver them—precisely because the Ukrainian troops have not been getting what they need.

Is President Zelensky corrupt? I suspect he is; Ukraine's politics have long been known for corruption. But whether he is or isn't doesn't impact my desire to help the people in Ukraine who are suffering. Since the beginning of time politicians across the globe have been corrupted, even in our own White House in Washington, DC. But I did not go to Ukraine to support Zelensky, Biden, or any other politician. I went to help innocent people.

The innocent people in Ukraine didn't ask for this. They are regular people who don't care much about politics; they care about their farms, their families, and their freedom. It's the same with the Ukrainian soldiers I've met. Most aren't even aware of the politics, and they're certainly not fighting in support of a certain regime. They're laying their lives on the line, because if they don't their homes, their livelihoods, and their families could all be destroyed—they are literally fighting for their lives.

Through all the static and political rhetoric, there is good and evil in this—and a lot in between. Putin is certainly evil, the people of Ukraine are good people, and there is a lot of corruption and gray area throughout. But when a global superpower unloads the full force of its military on innocent civilians, I don't think our first questions should be about politics. I believe that when innocent lives are being taken, the most urgent question that needs answering is this: Can I do something to help? And if the answer to that is yes, and you have the capacity to step in, then how can you not?

If we let our politics get in the way of our compassion for people in need, then we should probably change our politics. I have always been motivated to do what I can to help those who can't fully help themselves, and I am proud that my team and I decided to act. I have seen with my own eyes the evidence of Putin's barbarity in Ukraine, from mass graves filled with the bodies of women and children to clear evidence of the use of chemical weapons on civilians. I've never once doubted that going into Ukraine was the right thing to do. But I do have serious questions about the motivations and hidden agendas of the politicians involved. They know war crimes have been committed, yet they allow this war to drag on, coaching from the sidelines by throwing tens of billions of dollars and military equipment at the problem like fuel on a burning village.

The main issue is that the very politicians who have the ability to end the war in Ukraine are—ironically—the ones who have the most to gain from it, politically and financially. The money involved only provokes and prolongs a bloodbath, with hundreds of thousands of innocent lives being the consequence, while impacting global security and economic markets. Yet the power-broker political elites appear to be doing nothing to end the conflict.

People talk about the risk of the war in Ukraine sparking World War III, but in my opinion we're already there. Nearly thirty countries are involved—including Russia, America, China, Iran, and even North Korea. US drones and rockets are killing Russian troops, while Iranian drones are killing Ukrainian troops. This is a recipe for disaster on a global scale, and while the wrong world leaders will provoke war and bloodshed, the right world leader could conversely lead a ceasefire and encourage successful peace talks to end this proxy World War III.

The president of the United States does have the power and ability to swiftly end this war. There is no need for America to fight a proxy war against Russia at the cost of these innocent people, spend billions of US tax dollars, or instigate such a global catastrophe. What the president and leader of the free world should do is lead—lead through strategy, compassion, and strength.

A strong America with a strong president who is willing to impose sanctions still has global influence. Especially over Russia, whose economy is reliant on the rest of the world buying its energy exports. It's exactly what President Ronald Reagan did at the end of the Cold War:

he crippled Soviet premier Mikhail Gorbachev financially through economic warfare that targeted the sale of Soviet oil and gas.

Furthermore, with the clear evidence of war crimes in Ukraine, the leader of the free world has the ability to demand a ceasefire and lead a NATO coalition to usher in humanitarian aid for the Ukrainian people. Once NATO is there, Russia could not continue the assault. Putin is evil, but he isn't stupid. He would not risk an Article 5 NATO violation. A NATO humanitarian effort on the ground in Ukraine could remain until peace and compromise are found.

All it takes is for those with power to ask themselves the same question that my team and I asked: Am I going to sit on the sidelines and observe, or is it within my power to help? In times like these, it is up to all of us—politicians included—to do the right thing.

PROLOGUE

THREE BATTLES AT ONCE

Seaspray and I had been there for almost an hour. Parked near an abandoned building in the shadow of a tree line, on a muddy road sixty miles inside territory that had only just been liberated from the Russians. We weren't alone. The head of the Ukrainian police and a small crowd of Ukrainian soldiers were gathered around our 70 Series Toyota Land Cruiser.

All of them were staring intently. Say what you like about Elon Musk, but having one of his Starlink satellite receivers bolted to the top of our SUV had been a game changer for us. There's nothing like free Wi-Fi to win hearts and minds, especially when it's ten times faster than what I get back home in Texas. As the soldiers logged on and traded messages with loved ones far away, their war-weary faces relaxed. They were even happier when we opened the back doors of the cruiser and revealed the thousand-dollar espresso machine that was ratcheted down in the floorboard. Our mobile internet café was all we needed to make new friends and get the access to move forward on our mission.

But even though the soldiers were smiling, they were still alert. We all were.

Seven months of war had taught everyone involved that vigilance was vital to survival. And here, on the outskirts of Izyum, there was plenty to remind us of the danger. The area had been recaptured from the Russians only days earlier, and Putin's men hadn't gone far. Already that day Seaspray and I had seen nearly one hundred dead or dying Russian soldiers, plus enough abandoned military equipment to destroy a small city. The muddy roads were littered with T-54/T-55 and T-90 tanks, BTR-80 armored personnel carriers, ZSU-23–4 anti-aircraft guns, and BM-21 mobile missile platforms, all of which had either been taken out by the advancing Ukrainians or partially destroyed by the Russians themselves as they'd pulled out. There were rumors that the Russians hadn't retreated—they'd *fled*. Some had bugged out on foot, some on stolen bikes.

The invading troops had been pushed back, but they were clearly not giving up yet. According to Vadim—the head of the Ukrainian police who was accompanying us on the mission—there were still thousands of Russians close by, and the latest intel suggested they were currently on three sides of our position.

I had no reason to doubt it. Just hours earlier we'd seen a pair of Russian MIGs zip over us, dropping their ordnance on a target so close that we could see the fireball plumes as they exploded. From everything I'd seen in the months I'd spent in Ukraine, the MIGs' target could have been either military or civilian. The Russians weren't worried about civilian casualties; instead, they were actively seeking them out.

The previous day we'd visited mass graves—whole sections of forest cleared of trees with long, deep pits carved out of the soil and filled with bodies—with as many as fifteen hundred people in each. Nearly all that I saw were women and children with their hands bound behind their backs. They had all been shot in the head. Some of the bodies had been burned, or at least someone had attempted to set fire to them—which is what people do when they want to cover up a mass execution. But bodies don't burn well. Crimes like that are hard to hide.

Having seen those mass graves, I appreciated having a few moments to pause and think and pray while we waited in our Land Cruiser at the side of the country road. But the quiet buzz around our little internet café was interrupted when Seaspray's phone rang.

In addition to gathering evidence about possible war crimes committed by Russian troops, we were looking for a wounded and captured US Marine. America wasn't in the war—not officially at least—but my guess was that as many as four thousand former US servicemen were doing what they could in Ukraine. Some—like the Marine who had been caught by the Russians—had come to fight. Others, like Seaspray and me, had just come to help. We carried no guns and rode around the country in our specially modified vehicle, rescuing people who couldn't rescue themselves and providing the Ukrainian troops with whatever support we could. Sometimes that was as simple as free medical supplies, some of the fastest free Wi-Fi on the planet, and a double-strength espresso.

Seaspray's call didn't last long. "They lost comms," he said. "Nobody knows where he is now."

It was not the news either of us wanted to hear, and the Marine's chances of rescue were now practically zero. But there wasn't time to discuss it. Almost immediately we heard the familiar whistle of incoming Russian artillery, followed by the devastating *whumff* as it exploded behind us, shaking the ground beneath our feet. Then, seconds later, another one—this time even closer.

The troops scattered and Seaspray and I took cover next to the nearby building. Another round came in. Then a third. And a fourth.

The indirect fire was getting nearer with every explosion. Soon it was close enough to our position for us to see the clouds of dirt spraying out from the blast. It was heavy artillery, the kind where every impact sends a blast of pressure that rattles through your body, shakes your brain, and takes the air from your lungs.

Neither Seaspray nor I spoke. Unarmed and protected by only level-four ballistic vests and Gatorz ballistic eyewear, we pinned our backs to the wall and watched carefully as the Ukrainian soldiers organized themselves to repel the attack. None of them appeared anxious, but the

Russian fire got closer still—so close that the Ukrainians engaged in small-arms fire and I could hear the sound of the AK-47s' springs functioning as they fired. The Russians couldn't have been more than one hundred yards away. Maybe closer.

After a while, Vadim peeled back to where we were.

"They closed in behind us," he said, urgent but calm. "They are 360 degrees—all around us, but we will fight our way back out."

Vadim ran back to join the soldiers while Seaspray and I stayed where we were. Eight deployments to Afghanistan had put me in plenty of sketchy situations, but this was different, and not just because Seaspray and I were unarmed. In Afghanistan I'd been on the side of a major military power facing tribal Taliban terrorists, but what we were experiencing in Ukraine was uniform on uniform, country on country, with all the arsenal of modern-day weaponry on both sides—and Russia had control of the air. In other words, this was a level of threat like nothing I'd ever experienced before.

Yet despite the bullets and artillery cracking the air all around, I felt peaceful and calm. A quick glance at Seaspray told me he was feeling the same way. The Ukrainians were clearly dominant, and whatever Russian force was attacking us, it was likely just a remnant: a handful of men who thought they could be heroes, or Russian Vatniks willing to fight till the end. If they didn't escape or surrender quickly, they'd soon be dead.

With nothing else to do, I decided that now was a good time to talk to my son, so I pulled out my phone. Hunter's a Marine combat veteran, too, the third-generation Marine in our family. He was also in Ukraine but a couple of hours away in Bakhmut on a separate mission delivering medical supplies to frontline troops. At first I'd been reluctant to bring him over, but I'd seen him thrive out here. He'd become an invaluable member of the team, and I was proud of him. Even so, I wanted to hear his voice. I wanted to know he was okay.

"Hunter?"

"Dad! I—"

Before he could finish, another round of artillery landed close by our position.

"Was that incoming, Dad?" Hunter sounded a little concerned. More concerned than he needed to be.

"We're taking indirect fire. It's okay, though. They've got it under control. Seaspray says hey. How's it going?"

"I'm . . . hold on."

I listened as he shifted the handset. It wasn't clear what was going on at his end of the line, but I could just make out a car engine straining, hear the quick changes of gear and a vehicle thundering over rough terrain.

"Hunter?"

Then I heard it. The exact same sound that was occurring where I was. Artillery.

"We're taking indirect fire, too, Dad. Don't worry. I'm driving like a bat out of hell! We're good. I'll call you when we're clear."

He ended the call before I could say anything.

My sense of calm vanished. My heart rate climbed. Whatever was happening on these country roads outside Izyum, it was nothing compared to the battle that had struck up within me. Fear was on one side, faith on the other.

I closed my eyes for a moment, called out my prayer.

"I trust you, God . . . but please . . ."

ONE

NEVER FELT SO HOPELESS

I slept in late and woke up to an empty house. Kathy was out already, taking the dog for an early walk. I poured my first coffee but ignored my phone. I left it, untouched, on the counter and settled on the couch. Everything around me was peaceful, but on the inside I was dry and cracked. A drought had been wearing me down for weeks. Maybe even months.

I tried reading my Bible, but it was a struggle to concentrate on the words. Praying was even harder. Even draining my second cup of coffee didn't seem to help much. That drought within had unsettled me. I was beginning to sense a powerlessness in every area of my life—a feeling I'd battled with years ago. I knew it wouldn't be good for me to go back there.

After I'd been awake for an hour, I couldn't put it off any longer. I took a breath. Picked up my phone. I had to face the messages that I knew would be waiting for me.

There was a time before all this, a time when there was nothing remarkable about my first glance at my phone. Back then, I'd stare through bleary eyes at the messages waiting for me, my finger lazily scrolling up and down the screen as I slowly woke up. There would always be something to make me smile, often something to make me frown. Sometimes there would be problems to deal with too, but they were always manageable. There was never this flood, never this sense of feeling so hopeless.

I can tell you precisely when it changed.

April 14, 2021.

The moment that President Biden announced the total American withdrawal from Afghanistan, I knew it would be a disaster. Having served eight tours in the country as a Force Recon Marine and DoD contractor on a Special Operations Task Force, I knew the withdrawal would affect the future of America on a global scale and place at risk the thousands of Americans and allies who would eventually be left behind for slaughter. And it didn't take long for my phone to confirm it.

The first messages had come from Aziz, my friend and former interpreter. He had worked on our task force for nearly fifteen years and as a result had become a high-value target for the Taliban. In 2016 Aziz had applied for a Special Immigrant Visa (SIV), hoping to relocate with his family to the US in return for his years of service, but a process that was supposed to take nine months was still ongoing six years later. Aziz was stuck in Afghanistan, and when the White House ordered our troops to pack up and leave after twenty years, my friend knew full well that if someone didn't help him soon, he, his wife, and his six children would all end up dead.

The closer we got to the withdrawal, the more frantic Aziz's messages had become. He told me how he had taken his family on the run, moving from house to house every few days in a desperate attempt to stay one step ahead of the Taliban. Aziz wasn't just my interpreter of eight deployments; he was my friend. I held his children as babies and lived in his home. He'd saved my life multiple times and I'd done the same for him. There was no way I could leave him and his family there. So I did everything I could think of to help—reaching out to contacts, lobbying politicians, anything to speed up his visa process—but it was no use. Nobody could help. Everyone's hands were tied by the White House and the State Department. Aziz and his family were stuck. Their fate appeared to be sealed.

Eventually I joined with some friends and formed a coalition effort to do what our government wouldn't: the right thing. Against all odds, and thanks to the divine providence of God, we were able to get Aziz, his wife, and their children safely on their way to the US.

But there were others left behind. Not just thousands, but tens and hundreds of thousands, all desperate to get out before their homeland was turned over to the evil that is the Taliban. For a few brief days the world watched as scenes of chaos and terror unfolded in real time at Hamid Karzai International Airport (HKIA) in Kabul.

We did what we could for them too. Working round the clock for ten days straight, our team was able to get twelve thousand people past the Taliban checkpoints, onto C-17 military and chartered civilian planes, and out of Afghanistan. After that we stayed and led a coalition effort to get another five thousand people out of a place called Mazar-e Sharif, and then I spent ten more days on the Tajikistan border with a single teammate and fellow Force Recon Marine sniper, Dennis Price. Each night we swam across the Panj River that marked the border with Afghanistan, building routes out for thousands of women and children who were being blocked from evacuating by Taliban, Russian, and Chinese soldiers. It was one of the most incredible and horrific things I've been a part of—the result of extreme hard work, unbridled generosity, and the grace and favor of God. A miracle? Yes, I believe it was. But it was the kind of miracle God orchestrated due to good people saying, "Yes, send me," and trusting that he would have their backs when they went.

Five months had passed since then. The media had moved on, but the work was far from complete. Many of the seventeen thousand people we had been able to get out were still waiting in limbo, killing time in temporary facilities in the United Arab Emirates (UAE) while they waited for the US State Department to process their applications. We had rescued them from the Taliban, but they were now suffering the slow suffocation of bureaucracy.

Then there were the people we had left behind, people who, like Aziz, had risked everything to support our military over there. The thousands we had rescued were just a drop in the ocean compared to the masses who were stuck in Afghanistan. There, in the land that our government had walked away from, evil reigned again. Those eight tours that I'd spent working clandestine operations and living with the Afghan people throughout the country had taught me plenty about the brutality and barbarity of the Taliban. I knew full well what they would do with anyone they suspected of being supportive of America.

For the people stuck in the UAE who were running out of patience, and their countrymen trapped in Afghanistan who were running out of time, I was someone they hoped would help. Their desperate pleas came at me nonstop. Instagram, Facebook, and WhatsApp brought in tens of thousands of messages each week, and I was getting at least fifty emails per day. Every person had a story to tell, a story that broke my heart.

Uncle Chad, Uncle Chad, they would write. *Please help me. My husband was just killed. It is just me and my daughters now. We don't know where to go or what to do. The Taliban is going to take both my daughters. Please help!*

Often these messages came with pictures of children holding signs.

Uncle Chad, please save us. Uncle Chad, don't leave us here to die.

Others, especially those waiting in the UAE, would ask me why I had forgotten about them, begging me to press their case with the State Department.

Why did you bring us out only to let us rot?

Why are you not able to do what you promised?

What they didn't know was that I was stuck too. We had worked closely with the State Department during the rescues, following the strict protocols they had laid out for each and every one of those seventeen thousand people. But while we had delivered on our end, the State

Department's rate of progress had fallen off a cliff. I felt as though I had no power, no influence there. I was on the phone all the time and making regular trips to Washington, DC, to support those who hoped to come to the US—many of them under the SIV that Aziz had spent so many years chasing. Now that those people were no longer valuable, my government chose to abandon them. I was getting the impression that the State Department saw what we had done in the rescues as a potential political embarrassment. We were a clear reminder of the disastrous consequences of their flawed decision to surrender Afghanistan to the Taliban. We were simply making the White House look bad.

So every morning I was waking up and bracing myself for the avalanche of messages I would receive. With so much still to do to help those we had rescued, I had to triage. I had no choice but to ignore anything that wasn't directly addressed to me, so I'd made the decision to not look at Facebook or Instagram and only read messages that came in on my personal email, WhatsApp, or Signal. That still meant I was reading at least a hundred messages a day, each one with a compelling, urgent need that I wanted to fix. But most of the time I couldn't help them. The Taliban had blocked off almost all the routes out that we had developed and used previously, and the State Department was actively preventing us from getting anyone else into either the US or an ever-increasing list of other lily-pad countries. Even if we could get someone out of Afghanistan, there was nowhere we could legally take them.

It was the pictures that I found hardest to shake from my mind. We're not talking photos or anything particularly graphic. I'm talking kids' pictures, drawn with crayons on scraps of paper, then photographed and sent, lo-res and grainy, across the world. From the land of the enslaved to the land of the free. Skipping between satellites in a matter of seconds. Most days there would be a handful of them, many with the same stick-figure Taliban fighters, dressed in black like demons, with images of bodies on the ground in pools of blood. Whenever I looked at them, I wanted to scream. Nothing makes me so enraged as when I see innocent people, especially children, terrorized by evil men.

––––––––

Because of this constant barrage of messages, my mind was troubled, and my body felt the same. I wasn't eating right or taking care of myself, so my energy levels were way down. Plus, there was the problem of pain. The previous summer, when things were just starting up in Afghanistan, I'd picked up an injury while on the mats at my Brazilian jiu-jitsu (BJJ) school in Texas. I'd been grappling with one of my tough teammates, an upcoming MMA fighter, when I'd felt a pop in my groin. The pain had been instant, and an MRI confirmed that I'd torn one of my groin muscles clean off the bone. It happened just two days before leaving for the evacuations in Afghanistan, so I had decided against surgery and chosen to manage the symptoms instead.

Between my military service and my time as a pro MMA fighter, I've had my share of injuries. Working through the pain was nothing new, and I was confident that I could rehab without surgery. But five months after Afghanistan I was still deferring surgery and still in pain. The running, swimming, and rehab I was doing weren't making my groin much better, and my trips down to BJJ training weren't giving me much mental relief from the pressure I was under. Those young fighters two decades my junior didn't give me any free rides—nor should they. I'd trained a bunch of them and had taught them to take full advantage of any weakness in a foe. So when they saw the chance to grapple with me, their forty-six-year-old, fourth-degree black belt professor who was now drifting out of shape, they'd leap on it and come after me. I gritted through it, battling tooth and nail to keep up, but most times I'd leave training feeling worse than when I arrived.

Then there was stuff at home.

Besides feeling mentally overwhelmed by the challenge of helping so many people from Afghanistan, and not being physically where I wanted to be, I was not doing well with Kathy. We'd been married twenty-seven years and we'd been through some tough times together, including my battle with PTSD that almost drove us to divorce and me to suicide. We'd weathered that particular storm and grown strong as a result, raising three children into adulthood. We'd even written a book about marriage, *Fight for Us*, and it was due for publication in just a few weeks.

I didn't have the energy to promote it. And if I was honest with myself, I also felt unqualified at the moment to preach about healthy marriages. I was traveling so much, back and forth to DC, and even when I was home my mind wasn't focused on my wife like I should have been. I felt like a hypocrite.

Finally, there was me and God. I try to be disciplined spiritually, making regular quality time for prayer and devotions. But in the midst of that busy season, it had slipped. I wasn't spending anywhere near the amount of time I should have been with God, and I was paying the price. I had lost my sense of peace and grounding, and it had worn on me.

Mind, body, spirit, and family. There wasn't a single area of my life where I wasn't feeling the strain. And here's the thing that really did me in: I was supposed to know better. I was supposed to be some kind of expert on all this. After my life hit rock bottom in 2011 and I finally recovered from PTSD, Kathy and I founded a nonprofit to help other veterans. We called it Mighty Oaks, and in the twelve years since its creation it has grown considerably, having served over five hundred thousand warriors and spouses from the military and first-responder communities. Through our international efforts we've delivered resiliency programs in Europe and South America, and back in 2016 we began working in Ukraine. At the heart of our message is what we call the four pillars of resiliency—strength in mind, body, spirit, and social relationships. Every year I speak to tens of thousands of people about this. Yet here I was, struggling on every front, failing to take my own medicine. Every single one of my four pillars was weaker than it had been in years. I had little left to give. I was running on fumes.

———————

I was still on the couch when Kathy came back from her walk. Daisy the Vizsla did what she always does and leapt on me, attempting her dog equivalent of jiu-jitsu as she tried to pin me down. I wasn't paying her much attention. I was lost in my phone. For once, it wasn't anything to do with Afghanistan. Not directly, at least.

"Chad?" Kathy's voice was loud and clear, calling me back to her. "I said, what are you reading there?"

For months there had been reports in the press of unusual movements of Russian troops, first on its border with Ukraine, then in Belarus to the north. It was clear that Putin was up to something, and I'd been following the story closely. I put my phone down and apologized for not answering Kathy the first time. "Putin's flexing to see how Biden will respond," I said. "And I'm just wondering what Biden is going to do."

"Uh-huh?" Kathy gave me a look. "Doesn't Putin always do stuff like that? He's posturing, right?"

"No," I said. "I don't think he is. He's been watching us carefully. He knows we're weaker than we've ever been. He's planning something, and now he has a window. Biden's not going to show any strength and will cave, and Putin knows it."

"Hmmm."

Anyone who's been married as long as we have knows each other's noises, and there was no mistaking Kathy's response. It meant, *You're overthinking this one, Chad Robichaux.* It also meant, *How about you get off that sofa now and come give me a hug?*

I fully agreed with her about the hug. I kind of agreed with her about the politics. Or at least I wanted to be able to agree with her. I wanted to be wrong. I wanted to see Putin's movements on the border as nothing more than gamesmanship. But I couldn't. Thirty years around the military gives you a certain level of insight into the world. Experience sharpens your instincts and allows you to see the potential consequences of diplomatic actions. The way we had surrendered Afghanistan sent a clear message to the world: America's leaders no longer had the stomach for the fight. Our country was no longer a deterrent to hostility. When America is strong, the world is safe; when America is weak, the world is unstable. America was weak and vulnerable, and our enemies knew it. Putin knew it.

So when my phone soon started buzzing with news alerts, I was instantly sucked back into the world of geopolitics. The news was bad.

The Pentagon ordered all US troops in Ukraine to leave the country and reposition elsewhere in Europe.

It was a terrible decision. With as many as one hundred thousand Russian troops lining up on Ukraine's border with Russia in the east and with Belarus in the north, Biden was giving Putin a green light to move into Ukraine. True, the total number of US troops was small—just 160 members of the Florida National Guard, assigned to the 53rd Infantry Brigade Combat Team that had been deployed to Ukraine to train with local forces. They were small in number, and maybe not quite the most well trained that our country had to offer, but they were enough. The presence of those few troops was holding back the entire Russian army and serving as a deterrent to a Russian invasion of Ukraine.

With US troops in Ukraine, Putin knew that wounding any NATO service member—even unintentionally—would automatically trigger an Article 5 violation, resulting in the full force of NATO retaliation. By ordering the withdrawal of our troops, President Biden was setting a precedent for our allies to follow, ushering them toward the exits. With NATO representatives gone, he was opening the door for Putin to roll into Ukraine in a full invasion, leading to a bloody war costing hundreds of thousands of lives. A war that nearly thirty nations would become engaged in, creating what some would say is now a proxy World War III.

Finally, I put my phone away and went looking for Kathy. She was in our bedroom, watching the news.

I spent the rest of the day focused on my work. There was the usual list of calls to make—a list that would take me a whole week to get through—and the usual frustrations as I tried everything I could to make headway with the State Department. Throughout it all there were messages from people I'd never met, people who were stuck and terrified and who needed help. All along I had the same feeling of heaviness, the same fatigue, the same sense of being almost totally depleted. My internal drought wasn't showing any sign of ending any time soon.

The days that followed brought more of the same tasks, more of the same messages, and more of the same feeling of emptiness. On top of everything, Mighty Oaks was busier than ever, and my team needed me. The surrender of Afghanistan had left so many veterans discouraged and struggling with questions they couldn't reconcile. It had created a huge need for help, and we were receiving hundreds of new applications for programs. Life was busy, and the pressure was only increasing.

On February 14, two days after the announcement of the withdrawal of US troops from Ukraine, Biden flinched for a second time. He announced the closure of the US Embassy in Kyiv and evacuated the last of the American diplomats. After months of Putin's flexing on the border, it seemed inevitable that Russia would invade Ukraine.

That's when I got the call.

The moment I saw Sarah's name on my phone, I knew what she would be calling about. Sarah Verardo was a cofounder of Save Our Allies. This could only really be about one thing.

"You're going to Ukraine," she said.

"I am?"

"Yeah. Seaspray's there. He says the invasion's going to happen any day. We want you to be there to prepare for when it happens. Because when the invasion starts, we're going to want to be able to move people out."

We talked about details a little, and I told her I'd talk with Seaspray as soon as I could reach him, but there wasn't the need to say much more at that point. I could feel my heart burning with that old familiar feeling to take action and help, to serve. What I needed most of all was to get on my knees and pray.

I have a two-step process that I follow whenever there is a new opportunity ahead of me. I know that I like to go full steam ahead whenever there's good work to be done, especially in situations where there are innocent lives at risk and people in need who can't help themselves. But no emergency is so great, no opportunity so urgent that we should leave God out of the process and charge ahead on our own.

So first I pray.

I pray that God would place on my heart a clear burden for what He would have me do.

I pray for wisdom to discern the difference between God placing something on my heart and me just getting excited about launching myself into a new experience.

I pray for God to close doors that would lead me away from His will, no matter how appealing or exciting they might appear.

I pray that God might open the doors He would have me walk through, no matter how unlikely or unappealing those opportunities might appear.

I pray that God would help me remember that I'm not the savior of the world—He is.

I pray that God would help me get over myself and let go of the desire to form and follow my own plans, and instead get on board with His.

I pray a lot.

But I also talk.

I talk to Kathy and I talk to my board of advisers and directors at Mighty Oaks as well as other key people I trust. I tell them what's going on, ask them to pray, and invite them to talk. They bring their questions, and I listen hard when they speak. And if we're all in alignment—and only then—I act. This is not about me dragging my feet or drawing out the process; it's a deliberate, necessary step that allows me to go forward with full confidence.

Two days after talking with Sarah, I'd done my thinking and talking and praying and was ready to talk to Seaspray. He was a little hard to get ahold of, but that's nothing new. Typically, he's not in the most cell-friendly of places.

Seaspray isn't like most people. I mean, he and I have a lot in common—we both served in special operations, and both find that God uses the skills we have acquired to serve Him—but even among the military community Seaspray is unique. It's not just that he's eccentric, with long hair and a fondness for wearing flip-flops and a poncho when most guys with his background dress in tactical clothing like they're on the cover of

Soldier of Fortune. Seaspray's unique because he's simply one of the most qualified people on the planet at what he does.

And what he does is incredible.

He was a Green Beret before going over to our government's premier intelligence agency to do paramilitary work. (You're going to have to fill in the blanks for yourself.) Where most military special operations units work as a team, Seaspray and I both come from backgrounds where we have worked in what's called a "singleton" capacity: working alone with local nationals, often in some of the most nonpermissive or hostile environments imaginable. And all of this experience has led Seaspray to be the best precision rescue operator I have ever seen. If anyone's trapped, stranded, or captured, Seaspray's the man you want to go get them.

He understands international laws, has an extensive global network, and has an unmatched ability to track down and rescue people who nobody else could even have a hope of locating, let alone extracting. All that and a genuine servant's heart to go into the darkest corners of the globe to save people who are trapped in war zones, stranded, held hostage, or imprisoned—he's the top of the list when the stakes are the highest. Like Liam Neeson's famous, cheesy line in the movie *Taken*, Seaspray has "a very particular set of skills," and he uses them to incredible effect.

We'd first met the previous summer when we joined forces during the Afghanistan evacuations. In true Seaspray fashion, he'd just showed up on the ground at HKIA, and we quickly partnered to save as many people as we could. During that time Seaspray made a truly selfless decision, walking away from one of the most coveted positions in government special operations—and a career he had worked his whole life for—to help people he had never met before in a country that isn't his own.

He was at ground zero of the chaos outside the wire of HKIA with the other handpicked members of our team, finding ways to smuggle people out past the Taliban and into the airport for extraction. Without him, the number of people rescued—seventeen thousand—would have been a lot lower. Seaspray is an example of the kind of people I'm humbled and honored to work with.

"Hey brother, when are you getting here?" he said when he was finally able to return my call. "Russia is going to cross. It's happening."

What makes special operations *special* is that you always look to do something that nobody else can do. It's not an ego thing; it's practical and pragmatic. If you're doing something that could easily be duplicated by anyone else, what's the point? So any planning of any operation always starts here with a clear question—which is exactly what I asked of Seaspray.

"What's the unique need that nobody else can do but we can?"

Seaspray paused a beat, then gave me his answer. "It's not going to be a mass evac like Afghanistan where we're moving thousands of people. Anyone can drive a minivan or a bus over the border from Poland and haul out a bunch of people. It's those who *can't* get out that need help."

"Injured? Sick? Incapacitated? Trapped Americans?" My brain was already firing.

"Yeah," he said. "I brought some diplomat's elderly wife back from a hospital in Kyiv, and I recovered three teenage girls who had just been adopted by American families but couldn't get out. The car line was days long and it was near zero degrees, so we had to walk all night in the snow through the forest into Poland."

I could picture it clearly. Three young girls, tired and scared, in pain from the cold, struggling to the border, unaware just how lucky they were to have Seaspray guiding them to safety.

"It's going to get bad quick," he said. "When kinetic combat starts, there are going to be people who should have got out already but didn't. We've got to build a capability to help."

It was clear: not just the unique need and the way that our training and experience could be put to use, but also how we could do it. We'd need vehicles and medics and comms equipment and a ton of other stuff. As soon as Russia crossed the border and invaded, the need for rescue would only increase. It would be challenging, expensive, and dangerous. There was no end in sight, with the distinct possibility that at some point the whole country could become overwhelmed by Russian forces.

"So," asked Seaspray, "You coming?"

In the days before our call, I'd been through my process of trying to discern whether this was an open or closed door for me. I'd prayed and talked and prayed and talked. My board at Mighty Oaks had asked good questions, listened carefully to my answers, and all given their blessing.

When I'd talked about it with Kathy, her reply had been less about logistics and more about the heart. I'd tried to explain to her the best way I knew how. "If a baby was choking to death right there in front of you, you'd jump up and save it, right?"

"Right," she said.

"And if a neighbor's house was on fire, you'd call 911, then make sure everybody was out, right? You'd even go inside if you knew you could save someone."

"Of course."

"Well, how far away does someone have to be before we lose our compassion to help them? Just because Ukraine's thousands of miles away doesn't mean we don't help. Not when we have the ability to."

"I get it," she said. Up to that point I'd been struggling to phrase it right, but she did get it and was on board for me to go.

"What about us?" I asked.

"We've got through way worse than this, Chad," she laughed. "You need to get over there and help. We'll be fine."

So by the time I was on the call with Seaspray, listening to him ask me whether I was going to join him in Ukraine, I was as sure as I'd ever been that this was something I was supposed to say yes to. This was a door that God had opened, an invitation to which my response was a loud and clear "Send me!"—just as I have a number of times throughout my life. It's a familiar call that God has put on my heart, and it seems like I'm hearing it even more clearly these days.

There was no doubt in my mind that I needed to go, but I wasn't naïve about the situation. Both Ukraine and Russia are well-known as hotbeds for corruption, so I had to be clear about my motives. I wouldn't be going in defense of a country—I'd be going to help the innocent people who couldn't help themselves.

I still felt dry. I still felt tired. I was still almost totally depleted and in need of a break. But since when had that ever been a reason to say no to God? As weak and underresourced as I felt, I knew that the opportunity to help was from God Himself. And if God was calling me, He knew all about how I was feeling anyway. If the door was still open, who was I to doubt God's power to sustain me as I walked through it?

"Absolutely, brother," I said to Seaspray. "I'm on my way."

TWO

FINDING COMFORT
IN THE COLD

MARCH 4, 2022
Krakow, Poland

Even as my plane landed and taxied to the terminal at Krakow–Balice International Airport, I could sense the cold. It was late afternoon, and the sun had almost set, but there was just enough daylight left to see the fog and the bare trees beyond the perimeter fence and the gloom that covered everything. It was how I'd always imagined what so much of Eastern Europe must have looked like in World War II. In the face of a fearsome, mighty enemy, even the sun appeared to have given up.

In the two weeks since Seaspray and I had spoken, Russia had invaded Ukraine. Putin's troops had started by streaming in from the east and the north, aiming to overrun Kyiv, overthrow Zelensky, and claim a swift victory. Those plans hadn't worked out quite as expected, and the strength of the Ukrainian resistance had shocked the world. But even though Putin appeared to have underestimated things, Seaspray had called it right. An estimated two million people had already fled Ukraine since the invasion only ten days prior. The mass exodus was happening and millions more were surging the borders to escape. The exit lines were days long and the fuel had run out, so many now found themselves stranded and struggling to endure the brutality of freezing temperatures and wind while traveling on foot.

At the airport I linked up with Roman, a Ukrainian/Russian national who I had brought on board through a trusted NGO partner. He'd been heavily vetted and was fluent in Russian, Ukrainian, and English. Together we headed to the Sheraton located in the center of Krakow, where Seaspray had based himself. He'd told me that he had one room filled wall to wall with equipment and another room for living in, although I don't think he'd slept there once. The Sheraton wasn't the best option, but Seaspray had arrived before the whole world showed up in Poland, and at times like this it's typical for one hotel to become the location of choice. All the NGOs, the media, and the overseas government representatives were staying at the Sheraton. It was pretty clear we'd need to relocate quickly to escape the crowd.

Seaspray wasn't at the hotel when Roman and I checked in, but the next day, early in the morning, I made sure we were down in the lobby when he returned. He was pushing an old woman in a wheelchair who was repeatedly wagging her finger at him, jabbering away in what I guessed was Ukrainian. She looked angry. He looked exhausted.

They weren't alone. There was another elderly woman with them who was looking lost and confused, as well as Bo, a special operations veteran who had worked with Seaspray a lot in the past. Bo's a very skilled medic, super professional, and the type of man who polishes up like Clark Kent. Most important, Bo has a genuine heart to help people. It was my first time meeting him, and I could tell he was worn out both physically and emotionally. It was easy to recognize. I'd been there a hundred times myself.

"What's up, guys?" I said, walking up to them. Up close they looked even worse. Both of them were dirty, and their eyes looked like they hadn't had a decent night's sleep since I last spoke to Seaspray on the phone. And they stank, bad. "Good trip?" I asked. "You guys smell like a bag of rotten buttholes."

"Good enough," Seaspray smiled. We embraced and Bo and I shook hands and introduced ourselves. I introduced Roman to them, and he and I took care of the ladies so they could check into a room, get a shower and meal, and wait for their families to arrive to collect them. The old woman was still jabbering, but at least now Roman could hear her grievances and explain to her that her family was on the way to be with her.

Once the ladies were okay, Seaspray and Bo came down to grab a bite to eat and discuss plans for the next phase of operations, but they were both too wiped out to do much talking or planning.

"You rest up," I said. "I'll get myself acclimated to things and we will pick up later."

I figured it would take at least a day for Seaspray and Bo to recharge, so I decided to spend my first full day exploring Krakow. I knew exactly where I wanted to go first. It was the train station, one of the main arrival points for many of those fleeing Ukraine.

The concourse was full of people. Dressed in their warmest clothes, surrounded by bags and cases and shopping carts full of possessions, using any available power outlet to recharge their cell phones. Hardly any of them were looking at the departures board, and if anyone was talking it was only ever with low, quiet voices. Most of them were just sitting. Waiting. Breathing. Scared. Waking up to the fact that there was no next step for them.

I've been around refugee programs before—in Africa as well as other parts of the world—and there was something instantly familiar about the people gathered in the train station. I guess the trauma of being forced to leave your home and your homeland is so deep and fundamental that it makes people respond in similar ways. Parents hold their children tighter, children let themselves be held. Both of them keep their eyes open, alert to any possible danger. There is so much uncertainty and fear that you can not only see it, you can practically feel it in your soul.

But there was something about the people who had arrived in Krakow that was different from any other mass exodus I had witnessed. President Zelensky had recently ordered that all males of fighting age were barred from leaving the country, so there were no men waiting on the concourse—at least no man between the ages of sixteen and sixty. As I walked among the groups of women, girls, and boys, I couldn't help thinking of all the fathers, husbands, and sons who were left behind.

When we'd spent a while at the station, Roman took me to a community hall nearby where the local Polish Girl Scout troop had set up a refugee center of their own. Like the station, it was full of women and children and piles of baggage, but unlike the station, it was also full of noise and cots and the smell of freshly cooked food.

"This is Sasha," said Roman, introducing me to one of the Girl Scouts serving food. "She's doing great work here."

Sasha paused for a second to say hi, then went back to serving a line that must have been almost three hundred people long. She was wearing her Girl Scout uniform and couldn't have been much older than fifteen, but she had a presence about her that radiated maturity, love, and grace.

Roman and I sat and watched for a while. It felt different in the hall than it had in the station. People seemed just a little less fearful, a little less on their guard. I guess that when the Girl Scouts are in charge and doing such a great job, any stress is likely to ease just a little.

Watching the crowd as they collected and ate their food, I was struck by another difference between these refugees and those I'd met before. Without their winter coats on, people looked just like the folks at home. This was my first time seeing refugees in a First World country, and they looked just like the people from my neighborhood, just like the people I lived among. If it wasn't for the buzz of Ukrainian being spoken, I could easily have been in some church meeting attended by Kathy and her friends. And while the whole of Ukraine had lived in Putin's shadow, especially since his invasion of Crimea and the Donbas in the east in 2014, these people Sasha and her team of teenage girls were serving were no more prepared to flee their homes than you or I would have been.

I could feel my compassion grow.

When they'd finished serving, I asked Sasha if we could pray with people. She agreed, and so Roman and I spent as long or as little with people as they wanted. I didn't have any magic words to say and didn't expect to take away the pain or fear. Mostly I prayed that they would know that God loved them and that He was going to be with them every step of the way—especially in the middle of so much hardship. A lifetime of being around people who are living in the shadow of war has taught me that's the best way to pray.

We were almost done when an older lady came and sat down with us. She said that she was one of the Girl Scouts' leaders and that she was from Krakow. She also said that she was scared.

"When Russians invade," she said in halting English, "border will be Poland. No more Ukraine to keep Putin back. Russian troops at our door."

"I don't think it will come that far," I said quickly. I didn't have any evidence to base it on, but my heart went out to her.

She gave me a look that told me she understood perfectly what I had said, but that she also thought I was just plain wrong. "When Russia come, will America help?"

I thought back to the previous summer, to Biden's decision to withdraw those 160 National Guard troops and shut the embassy in Kyiv. If I was going to give her my honest answer, it wouldn't have eased her fear. So I chose to offer comfort instead.

"If that ever happened, there's enough compassion and courage in America and among her allies to come in and drive Putin all the way back. But what I really want to say to you is that it's okay that you feel scared right now. It's normal to feel fear when war is close by, but look around. We are all here for each other." We left a little while later and made our way back in the direction of the hotel, walking along elegant Eastern European streets where Ukrainian flags hung high on the red-brick buildings above. I'd noticed the flags before, but as I walked it struck me just how many there were. The whole of Krakow was opening its doors to its neighbor.

We had not gone far from the refugee center when I saw a shop that was just closing up and decided to duck inside. It was a florist, and the instant Roman and I walked in I was transported a million miles away from the world of war and fear and calculations about Putin's next move.

"Do you speak English?" I asked the young woman behind the counter.

"Uh, yeah," she said, giving me a *dumb American* look and sounding like she'd just spent a year in California.

"Great. I'd like to buy some flowers, please."

The *dumb American* came back stronger. "O-kay. What do you want?"

"A lot. As much as my friend and I can carry."

When she figured out that I was serious, she showed me what she had left and started gathering bunches on the counter.

When she was done and I'd paid, she asked me, "How come you want all these?"

I told her about the refugee place back near the station. "I figure they could do with something nice in their lives right now."

She smiled, then added a load more bunches onto the counter.

When we got back to the refugee center, Sasha was serving the evening meal. She guessed what we were doing right away and nodded to us to have at it. I felt a little reluctant, even fearful about what the women might think. Would they be scared, offended, or question our intentions? I asked Roman what he thought, and he immediately brushed off my concerns and said they would be happy, so we proceeded.

For the next hour we walked around the room, picking our way between the cots, handing out these beautiful individual flowers to each lady and child. We didn't say much, just handed them over with a smile.

By the time we'd finished, the whole room was starting to smell just a little like the florist shop. Some of the women were smiling, some laughing, and some started crying as soon as they took them. A few were just lying on their cots, eyes closed, tender arms embracing the flowers and smelling them. Roman was right—my fears were in my head, and in a time of such sadness we were able to be part of a moment of joy and hope, with something as simple as a flower.

———

Seaspray and Bo were both still in recovery mode the next morning, so Roman and I drove out to visit the other location that was high on my list: the Polish/Ukrainian border.

It took three hours to reach Border Crossing Six from Krakow, but in that time we slipped into a whole new world.

It was way colder here than back in the city. The air carried with it the kind of frigid feel that forces you to keep moving. The sky was gunmetal gray, the wind fierce, and the rain nonstop. It must have been twenty degrees or cooler, and it defied physics that the temperature could be so low but it was still raining instead of snowing.

Looking through the crossing into Ukraine, I could see a line of cars disappearing into the distance as people waited to get into Poland. I'd heard varying reports of how long the line was: some said five miles, others said twenty. One person had told me people were waiting five days. However long it was, it was barely moving. The cold alone was a serious threat to life, and if Putin decided to, he could easily carpet bomb the whole line from the air. In a matter of seconds, the death toll could be in the tens of thousands. But he wouldn't attack civilians like that, would he?

For every car I could see, there must have been at least ten people walking up to the border on foot. Some of them looked like they'd abandoned their cars farther back down the line. Others looked like they'd been walking for days. As I stared, my eyes landed on a family of four plus a dog pausing near the border. The parents were young, maybe late twenties, and the kids were preschoolers. The dad was hugging them all, saying his goodbyes. It was too cold for anyone to linger, so as soon as he was done and had watched as his wife, kids, and dog joined the line to cross into Poland, he turned around and started walking back along the line of cars. Walking back to war.

On the Polish side of the border, the expressions on the faces of those who had just crossed told of their journey so far. Exhaustion, relief, sorrow, confusion, fear, and hope—many people displayed them all. Their shoes and clothes soaking wet, they dragged their luggage through the rain, blue fingers holding the handles, blue lips biting back the tears.

There must have been ten thousand refugees there, but something amazing was happening among them. As soon as people crossed over they immediately found themselves surrounded by hundreds of volunteers, NGOs, and kindhearted people who had turned up to help. Drivers were waiting with empty passenger seats, offering a ride anywhere people wanted to go. Others were handing out warm coats, cell phones, and SIM cards. There were oil drums filled with burning wood for people to warm themselves by, Sikhs in their turbans serving bowls of delicious-smelling curry, and NGOs offering medical care. Good people from all over the world and all sorts of backgrounds had shown up in the midst of crisis to care for their fellow man. It was nothing less than beautiful to see so much unity, especially in the Jewish NGO's medical center staffed by a volunteer team of German medics.

I recognized most of the names of the nonprofits who had shown up, and many of them were from the Christian community, but not one single government was represented there. Not one.

Part of me was in assessment mode—analyzing what I was seeing, trying to figure out how we could be the most effective in our help. But part of me just needed to wander among people, feeling the ebb and flow of so many emotions. Whatever was coming next, however we ended up helping, I wanted to do so from a place of compassion.

Back when I had been active military, success was easily defined in terms of targets located and eliminated from the battlefield. Having spent the previous decade building Mighty Oaks and moving into the world of nonprofits, I was still learning to adjust my ideas about success. Efficiency and professionalism still mattered, and reaching our desired outcomes was important, but the main thing was following God's lead to serve others. And to do that, I needed to keep my heart open to being stirred by the things that stirred His.

From the moment I'd arrived at the border, I'd been able to hear music. At first I thought it was a playlist of solo piano tunes, but as I got closer to the source, I realized it was live—a man, younger than me, sitting at his grand piano right in the middle of all the chaos.

I joined the small crowd gathered to listen. I didn't know the names of all the pieces he was playing, but when the first few notes of "Imagine" by John Lennon started, I recognized them instantly.

I stood, transfixed, and inhaled deeply. The music was beautiful, and for a while the rain and the twenty-degree weather faded.

When the piano player paused to warm his fingers, I asked for his story.

"I came to help," he said.

"Where are you from?"

"Germany. When I saw the pictures of people crossing, I knew I had to come. So I pulled my piano behind my car to get here. They have been hearing bombs and rockets. I wanted them to hear something beautiful as soon as they reached safety."

When his fingers had warmed up he went back to playing, and I walked off to find a medical NGO that had made contact a few days earlier, asking if they could accompany us when we crossed the border. As I walked I thought about everything I'd seen so far—especially among those who had come to help. Cooking a couple of gallons of curry, handing out free winter coats, playing a piano in the icy rain—none of these were particularly difficult things to do, and yet out here on the edge of war, they were deeply powerful acts. They brought light in the darkness, hope in the face of fear. They were simple acts done with great love, just the way God desires for us to serve one another. In the midst of evil, it hit me that God had to be smiling at the kindness and selflessness of these people.

I found the NGO working out of a field hospital and walked inside. It was busy in there, with at least a dozen people huddled in small cubicles where they were being treated for hypothermia, foot problems, and other injuries picked up on the long walk to the border. Someone was sobbing almost hysterically in a screened-off section toward the back. I introduced myself to one of the medics and was told to wait while the team leader finished up with someone.

The sound of the person weeping gradually eased, and eventually the doctor I was waiting for emerged from the back.

John Cooper was my age, American, and had the air of someone who'd been in places like this before. I knew a little of his bio—he was a former US Navy surgeon who had worked in CSH (Combat Support Hospitals) on the battlefields of Iraq and Afghanistan. He had chosen to come to Poland to see if he could provide emergency medical care for those crossing. He'd been there only a few days, but he was clearly disturbed by what was going on.

"We're seeing a lot of people like that," John said quietly, nodding in the direction of the back cubicle where the woman was still crying. "She

35

was held captive by Russian soldiers, who killed her husband and then raped her repeatedly over a few days. She said that the soldiers forced her children to watch."

He paused and we both sat in silence.

"What gets me is their strength," he continued. "They've been through such trauma, but they don't crumble. They keep it together long enough to reach the border and get their kids to safety. It's only when they get here and realize they're safe that they let go like this."

We talked a while about the difficulties John was facing on the border. He'd arrived in Poland offering his services but had quickly found that he wasn't going to be granted a license to work here. At best, all he could administer was basic first aid and try to comfort people. He was another powerful example of human kindness in action, helping people he didn't know from a country he'd never visited, with no expectation of reward. We expressed appreciation for what he was doing and moved on.

------◆------

By the time I made it back to the hotel in Krakow, Seaspray and Bo were rested and ready to get to work. Along with Roman, we all met in Seaspray's second room, which looked more like an REI warehouse than a five-star hotel. There was stuff everywhere—backpacks and hiking sticks, night vision goggles and radio equipment, and at least a dozen pairs of boots and shoes for different occasions. When I'd taken it all in, Seaspray gave me a look that said, *I didn't know what to bring, so I brought it all.*

I shifted a box of Mountain House MREs and sat on the bed.

"Roman and I went to the border," I said. "Crossing number six."

"Crazy, isn't it?" said Seaspray.

We talked a little about what I'd seen there, but moved on quickly to what we could do to help. Since nobody was doing mobile medicine in Ukraine, we decided to start there: moving people who couldn't move themselves. Since Seaspray had already done a couple of these trips, he had a clear idea of the main risk we would face. Checkpoints had sprung up all over Ukraine, and navigating them wasn't easy.

"These checkpoints are mostly run by local militia guys who think they're king of the world," he said. "They're jumpy and wary of foreigners, so we're going to have to appear completely nonthreatening, all smiles and hands up and super relaxed."

We also wanted to be ready to meet any future need. The war was eleven days old and the situation in Ukraine was hard to predict. Putin's promise of a lightning-fast capture of Kyiv had failed, but if we knew one thing it was that anything could happen. We needed to be ready, so our conversation lasted long into the evening. We tried to put ourselves in Putin's position, hoping to figure out what his next move might be. We played out all kinds of scenarios, from his Kyiv offensive succeeding and the capital falling to Russia attacking any of the country's nineteen nuclear power plants and reactors, resulting in anything from power shortages to a full-scale nuclear catastrophe. We discussed the possibility of those miles-long lines of people waiting to cross the border becoming a target, or Putin deciding to take out the major bridges. There were dozens of high-vulnerability points across the vast country, and anything could happen.

There were also a lot of NGOs already working in Ukraine as well as on the border. Between the four of us we had contacts with almost all the faith-based NGOs, and so we were able to piece together a detailed overview of just how vital a role they were playing. While the politicians were making speeches, it was the NGOs who were really preventing the Russians from winning. They were the ones making sure the refugees at the border were being cared for, who were delivering the essential supplies that the Ukrainians needed—from fuel to food and medical essentials. This certainly made the NGOs an enemy of Russia and a resource that Putin would have to target to be successful. The main question for us was whether the Russians would choose to attack the NGOs just like any other military target or take a more measured approach by trying to cut off their ability to operate.

I don't know who said it first, but as soon as the word *communications* was mentioned, everyone's focus intensified and the conversation became a tumble of ideas.

"If Russia takes out the phone grid or the power grid, those NGOs will be in trouble."

"They won't be effective."

"And they'll be vulnerable."

"They don't have sat phones?"

"Not enough."

"Interesting."

"We could help with that."

"Set up an alternative communications grid?"

"Exactly."

"Get them the right equipment and teach them how to use it."

"Satellite phones and HF and VHF radios."

"Needs to be encrypted."

"And with solar-panel charging stations."

"It'd be complicated."

"And expensive."

The room paused.

"Since when was money ever a problem for God?" I said.

"If it's God's will, it's God's bill!"

THREE

A CHIP OFF THE OLD BLOCK

As soon as we'd agreed that we would focus on rescue operations and building a communications network, we moved into full execution mode. Everyone had their own task: Seaspray was coordinating with local nationals and government officials in Ukraine, Bo was working on other relationships to gather solid intelligence on threats, Roman was identifying supplies and vehicles, while I was on the phone collaborating with other NGOs and donors to build a coalition effort and raise funds. Some of the details about our work were still vague, but one thing was clear: we were going to need a lot of money if we were going to pull off this massive undertaking.

I started by putting in calls to a handful of people I have known for years. They share my passion for helping those in need, and they also have the means to write big checks to make things happen. To each of them I said the same thing: "If you want to help prevent World War III, I have a way you can help. I don't need money today, but I will soon. Just be ready." All of them came back with some version of the same response. "I'm ready."

We worked hard throughout that first day, but it didn't take long before we encountered our first problem—a clear reminder that even though we were hours away from the border with Ukraine, we were still a target.

It happened during a security sweep of our vehicles. Roman was searching under the driver's seat when he found something that looked out of place.

"Uh . . . what's this?" he asked Bo, holding up a strange little puck with wires hanging off it. "It was attached to the battery down here."

Bo recognized it instantly and brought the GPS tracker back to Seaspray's room. I don't think any of us were either particularly surprised or concerned by the knowledge that someone was following our movements, but it did push us to make a decision.

Ever since I'd arrived in Krakow the Sheraton had been filling up with people. All the media, NGOs, and every foreign government seemed to be represented there. In some ways it was useful to be able to bump into contacts in the lobby and get things done face-to-face, especially when it came to talking with the NGOs about how we could build them their comms packages. But there was a cost to it all. There were plenty of Russian-sounding people floating around, posing as media, and one woman in particular was making a habit of taking selfies with as many people as possible. Eventually she'd been called out and told to leave the hotel, but between that and Roman and Bo finding the tracker, we had all the confirmation we needed that the location was not secure. So we added another task to our already long list of vital, urgent jobs: we needed to find somewhere new to live and work.

It took a few days, but eventually we moved somewhere more suitable than the Sheraton. It was a cluster of properties in a gated compound on the outskirts of the city, and we were careful to set up cameras outside and put good security protocols in place. We designated one room to be our operations center, and I got a few large whiteboards to keep track of everything that Seaspray, Bo, Roman, and I had in motion. The more we discussed how we were going to work in Ukraine, the more items we added. Hour by hour, with each unique logistical challenge that we considered, the whiteboards filled up with items that we would need.

The biggest challenge we faced was the fact that moving around Ukraine at night was going to be difficult. In addition to the checkpoints all over the country, many areas were introducing strict nighttime curfews. About the only vehicles and personnel allowed to move with any kind of freedom were ambulances and medics, so we decided to buy ambulances and EMT clothing, and to create some official-looking IDs. Those items all went on the board.

We'd heard reports of Russian forces blowing up roads, so we assessed alternative options for moving people safely off-road. We hit the internet and found a six-wheeler modular truck that had been built for a motocross team. That went on the board too.

At some point we even got talking about the Ukrainian rail network, which the Russians seemed to be leaving alone for now but appeared to be a potential target. I found a unique vehicle that would allow us to drive both on roads and on rail tracks and added it to the list.

Within a couple of days there were a dozen different vehicles on my whiteboard, with a combined price tag approaching $1 million. I hit the phones, calling back the potential donors I'd already spoken with. Many were the people I'd turned to the previous summer to help with the Afghan evac, and most of them had been friends of mine for over a decade. There was a lot of trust there, on both sides, and within a week most of the money we needed was in hand and we were able to start buying the vehicles.

We immediately hit a hurdle. None of us were Polish citizens, and since we were not registered as an NGO in Poland, we were unable to fill out the paperwork required for the vehicles. The solution was Mike, Seaspray's brother-in-law. He was a Polish national and he was willing to help. Willing, though not entirely happy.

"They're going to think I'm a drug lord!" he said when we told him about all the vehicles we wanted to buy in his name. "The government is going to be all over me!"

He had a point, and I was concerned for a moment that he might have a change of heart.

"What do you want us to do?" Seaspray asked. "We need you."

"Okay, okay," he said, thinking for a moment. A long, uncomfortable minute edged by, but eventually Mike's face broke into a smile. "I love it."

We agreed to figure out how much tax he'd have to pay on the vehicles and give him the money. Then we went back to buying more vehicles.

Even though special operations training prepares you to look for the unique role you can play in any given situation, it also teaches you to be smart and use whatever resources are available. Being a lone wolf sounds cool, but there are good reasons why wolves in the wild operate in packs. So we were careful to keep good lines of communication open with the Polish and Ukrainian governments, as well as representatives from other NGOs, to make sure that we were operating with as much official consent as possible. We were even keeping our connections in the US government aware of what we were up to and liaising on how we could assist.

It paid off. Our contacts within the US, Polish, and Ukrainian governments were able to give us helpful information about the operational threat and environment on Ukrainian front lines. Most important, we learned that Russia had been sending its own special forces teams into Ukraine to identify possible targets and call in air strikes. These guys, mainly in their thirties and forties, were rumored to be athletic looking and confident, had been given blue American passports, and were wearing high-end adventure gear and posing as humanitarian workers. In other words, they looked exactly like us.

This was bad news, but it wasn't necessarily catastrophic. Seaspray had already told us how nervous some of the Ukrainians were on their checkpoints, and at least now we had a little more understanding why. Most of the country's makeshift checkpoints were manned by everyday citizens armed with hunting rifles, shotguns, and machetes. It was easy to imagine how nervous they would feel and how suspicious they would be of a bunch of middle-aged humanitarian workers like us. We now knew that these checkpoints were likely to be some of the biggest threats we would face, so aside from making sure that none of us would be wearing any of the particular brand of outdoor clothing that the Russians were rumored to favor, we also doubled down on the plan that Seaspray had first suggested—to be as nonthreatening and low-key as possible.

If you believe what you see in the movies, you'll assume that when people go undercover they're handed a manila envelope with a fake passport and an entirely new identity. The truth is nowhere near as exciting or as efficient. The basic principle of adopting a cover story is that it should be as close as possible to reality. The more you have to lie, the more likely it is that your story will unravel under scrutiny. So for us about to cross into Ukraine, posing as medics wasn't a big stretch of reality. All of us had received some form of mid-level medical training during our careers, and all the medical equipment that we were traveling with was going to be used to provide emergency medical treatment to those who needed rescue. We could happily pass ourselves off as a bunch of overseas EMTs who had come to Ukraine to help people, so there would be hardly any need to lie at all, which would make the whole thing a lot easier.

That being said, we did resort to a tried-and-tested method to make ourselves look a little more authentic. In addition to buying hi-vis florescent yellow jackets and covering all our vehicles with prominent red crosses, we created official-looking, laminated ID cards with a QR code that linked to our NGO's website. We also added a little extra flourish by visiting a local stationery store and getting a rubber stamp made for an organization we'd made up: the International Association of Humanitarian Services. We used the stamp on all the paperwork we had, making it look even more official. We also double-checked all the paperwork for our vehicles and ensured they were mechanically reliable and stocked with recovery kits to address any breakdowns.

Finding vehicles that would serve as ambulances was a challenge, but building the comms network and packages was proving to be a big undertaking as well. Seaspray and I had been putting together what's known as a PACE plan, where we would provide a Primary, Alternate, Contingency, and Emergency method of the NGOs maintaining contact with each other and the Ukrainians. After identifying restrictions, Russian capabilities, available equipment, and putting together a budget, we finally came up with a list of what each comms package should contain:

Iridium satellite radios with yearlong subscriptions—a reliable and extensive satellite network

Very high frequency (VHF) radios—for vehicle-to-vehicle communication

goTenna 264-bit encrypted, closed-loop network—allowing a group to create their own secure cellular mesh network and track each other's locations in real time

GPS units—so that we could track each package and be easily notified by any user if they got in distress

Gold Star solar panels and power banks—to keep everything working if the power grid went down

Each of these comms kits would cost over $10,000, and we initially hoped to build hundreds of them. I felt confident that raising the money wouldn't be a problem, but sourcing the equipment itself while in Poland proved problematic. Even if we could track all the components down and get them shipped across international borders to us, there was a good chance that our actions might come to the attention of the Russian security forces. Since someone had already been interested in us enough to track our van, we didn't want to draw any more attention to ourselves.

More important, we wanted the first comms packs to be ready to go within the next four to five days.

There was only one real solution to our problem, and that was to have someone buy the gear in the US and bring it over to Poland in person. And there was only one person I could think of who I trusted to tackle a task like that in such a short timeframe: my eldest son, Hunter.

Ours is a military family, and together we have over eighty years of service from World War II, Korea, Vietnam, and finally Afghanistan, where Hunter and I had both served. My father was the first Marine in the family, followed by myself and my two sons, Hunter and Hayden. We've always been close, and I count them my best friends. All of us have followed my father's footsteps, and Hunter served as an ANGLICO (Air Naval Gunfire Liaison Company) Marine assigned to Georgian Infantry on a legitimate combat deployment to Afghanistan in 2019, where he saw combat action. ANGLICO Marines are assigned in small four-man teams to our foreign allied partners in order to call in US air support and indirect fire onto the enemy. So two of the strengths of a Marine like Hunter are that he is great under pressure and that what little he doesn't know about comms equipment probably isn't worth knowing.

Hunter is his father's son with a servant's heart, and when he is focused on something, he works with a deep passion until it is fin-ished—a chip off the old block. When it came to putting the comms packages together, Hunter was just the guy to call. Of course, it wasn't quite as simple as that.

The previous summer, Hunter had played a key role in the mission to get Aziz and all those others out, but it was not quite the role he wanted. For obvious reasons our Center of Operations was in Abu Dhabi rather than Afghanistan. I was initially there along with Hunter and others from our team, coordinating with Seaspray and others on the ground as well as liaising with the State Department, NGOs, donors, media, and other foreign governments to get people out. When the opportunity came for me to head to Afghanistan via Tajikistan to locate and build routes out for thousands of women and children, Hunter desperately wanted to come along. I'd benched him and taken a guy named Dennis with me. A seasoned Force Recon Marine and one of the most respected Scout Snipers in special operations made Dennis the right guy for the job. I'd felt bad for Hunter, but I knew we were heading into a very dangerous area where I'd need to rely on my partner, not worry about him and try to protect him from harm. I needed to be focused on operating, not being a dad.

Hunter's an old soul and super smart, and he had taken it okay, but I knew it had hurt him. It had hurt me, too, seeing him disappointed like that. Months later when I left for Poland, the wound was still far from healed. When I'd first talked to Sarah and Seaspray about getting involved, we'd planned on a bunch of us from Mighty Oaks coming out to Poland. That plan hadn't worked out, and I ended up traveling out solo. Hunter had not said anything about it, but I knew he was sad that he hadn't been able to accompany me.

"Hunter?" I said when I called him from Krakow on Wednesday, March 9. It was 3:00 a.m. in Houston, but there was no time to waste. "You still want to be a part of this?"

"Sure. What do I have to do?"

"I'm sending you a list of comms equipment and a $300,000 budget. I need you to buy everything on the list. You're going to have to search the whole country to pull it off because this much stuff won't be in one place. Then you're going to get everything bagged up, fly it here, and turn around and fly home. It's not super sexy or anything, but I'm telling you, this is super important. This is literally an opportunity to change the course of history and how we help stop World War III."

"Okay," he said, calm as ever. "When do you need me to bring it to you?"

I paused for a moment. It was Wednesday already. "Saturday."

Hunter didn't skip a beat. "Okay," he said. "Send me the list."

I left Hunter to it and spent the next days deep in the work in Krakow. We added a couple more members to the team—Sean Lee, who was a former Army 82nd Airborne Soldier and who worked for Sarah, and Dr. Mike Simpson, who had served thirty years as a Green Beret, Airborne Ranger, and doctor on the premier special operations medical unit in the US military. Mike had a couple of other doctors with him, including Richard Jadick and Will Dutton.

We spent time meeting with a select few NGOs to tell them about the comms packages and update them on our medical rescue plans. There was a lot of interest, though we were careful who we spoke to, especially as a lot of the meetings were held back at the Sheraton.

Seeing guys on the payroll of the World Health Organization and the World Food Program lounging around the Sheraton's restaurant, feasting on steaks and red wine, while I knew for a fact that they were still doing nothing at the borders or in Ukraine itself, really boiled my blood. That was only amplified when someone working for one of the biggest government disaster-relief organizations asked if we could drive one of their trucks to the border next time we went. They wanted us to take a photo of it for their social media channels. I declined in such a way that they never asked something so atrocious again.

But the most surprising encounter happened when I met with someone from one of my favorite NGOs, Samaritan's Purse. Ken Isaacs is the vice president of international programs and government relations and one of the most compassionate, intelligent, and impressive people I have been privileged to work with. He was a big help to me personally in leading the Afghanistan evacuations. Ken took Seaspray and me to a meeting of church leaders, all of whom were connected to a different group of churches in Ukraine. In many ways it looked like every other church leaders' meeting I'd ever been to, with a bunch of guys of different shapes and sizes sitting around in a circle, taking turns to stand up and address the room about what they'd been doing. Only in this particular meeting there was no talk about congregation numbers, building programs, or outreach events. Here it was all about the war and what the churches within the network were doing to help people in need.

In just a few minutes I heard stories that left me amazed and inspired.

One guy spoke about how their church had been able to deliver a bunch of radios and medical supplies to frontline troops, smuggling them past Russian forces in the process.

Another talked about how an NGO had provided dozens of sets of high-grade body armor and how people from his church had got it in the hands of some soldiers just hours before they were attacked by Russian forces.

Someone else explained that one military commander had a bunch of troops with enough weapons but no socks. The local church had been able to get word to an American NGO, who jumped into action. Within less than forty-eight hours the church was able to return to the troops with boxes and boxes of quality socks.

As I listened, I discovered that it wasn't the NGOs alone who were helping the Ukrainian military. The truth was that the NGOs were only able to help the military because they had an incredible partner who was willing to take risks and be completely dependable. The Ukrainian church had formed its own underground network and was playing a vital role in getting the aid that the NGOs were providing across the country to the troops themselves.

The key to what was making the Ukrainian church so effective was trust. The leaders I heard speaking at the meeting were from a full range of denominations, from evangelical to Orthodox, and even though I had no idea what their relationship was like before the war, there was no sign of anything but openness and unity among them now. They trusted each other, and they were clearly trusted by the military.

After I asked Hunter to buy and bring out the comms equipment, he'd earned the nickname FedEx from the team. As I sat and soaked in the stories of the ways that churches were working, it hit me that they were doing on a national scale what Hunter was doing for us. They were ensuring that the essential, lifesaving equipment needed on the front lines was delivered safely and securely. From that moment on, in my mind, referring to Hunter as FedEx would only ever be a compliment.

Hunter walked through customs at Krakow airport at 2:00 p.m. on Saturday, March 12, somehow managing to push three trolleys with a combined total of fourteen bags. In a little under one hundred hours, he had been able to locate, acquire, pack, and personally courier over everything we had asked him to bring.

We hugged.

"I'm super proud of you, buddy," I said. Hunter just smiled, shrugged, and told me he felt the same about me.

We didn't wait long but hurried back to our safe house. We spent the short drive talking about how he'd been able to source all the items. Between the ongoing COVID supply chain issues and the events in

Ukraine, stock was low for high-grade comms equipment, and Hunter had ended up cleaning out REI's stock of GPS units and flying state to state scouring the country for iridium radios. Most amazing of all was how he'd not been questioned even once by any customs officials on his journey over from the US.

As soon as we arrived, the guys welcomed Hunter like one of their own. I could tell that he was touched when Bo said that he'd made up a cot for him and that Hunter should get some rest, and when Seaspray thanked him for a job well done.

"It's not like my old unit," he said to Bo and me quietly as he started unpacking the gear. "The lowest ranked always got the worst deal."

"Yeah, it's different here," Bo joked. "Just ask your dad. He's sleeping on the floor."

———

Hunter took a couple of hours to crash but was soon back downstairs, joining Seaspray and me. We were staring at the different piles of equipment, a total of over two hundred different items. Everything we had asked for was there, but as we stared it was dawning on us that we'd failed to develop a clear plan for how we would get everything ready to use. We knew what we needed, we knew how to make it all work, but we didn't have the hours, even days, needed to set up, program, and register hundreds of individual pieces.

"You want me to set it up?" asked Hunter.

Seaspray and I didn't need to discuss it.

Hunter set to work that very moment. It was obvious that he'd already been thinking about the process, and he was completely dialed in as he worked. There was no wavering, no having to start over because he made a mistake. He was just steady, methodical, and thorough as he changed parameters in the phones' settings, went online to register and set up each contract, then added the serial numbers in his spreadsheet before going outside and checking that the equipment worked. It was a complicated and meticulous process, and it took Hunter about thirty minutes to complete the first handset. I knew I would have been incapable of doing it that quickly. I also knew that Hunter getting all two hundred devices set up was a massive task.

"You good?" I said as he started on the second handset.

"Yeah," he said, his eyes narrowed. I'd seen that face so many times before—when he was little and learning to shoot his first rifle or figuring out how to reel in a red snapper when we went out fishing. It was the look of concentration and of confidence. Most of the time when he was growing up, he'd go from learning from me and asking lots of questions to teaching me how to do it better on the next trip.

We left him to it.

For three days solid he worked, pretty much without sleep. I resisted the urge to play dad and tell him to get some rest. I figured the last thing he needed was to be treated like a child.

When he'd finished setting up all the devices, he moved on to combining them into fifty different comms packages and setting up the software to track each one in real time. When he was done, we all gathered round the large flat-screen twin monitors that formed the operation center to watch his demo and hear him talk through how it all worked.

It was awesome.

Amid all the high fives and congratulations, Seaspray turned to me. "We're going to need someone to run all this now," he said quietly. "He did a good job here. I'm going to ask him to stay. That okay with you?"

It was fine with me. "He earned it. I'm not going to stand in your way."

Hunter took the news like a man with five times his experience. He nodded, said he'd be happy to stay on, then went right back to work. But I spotted the smile in his eyes.

<hr />

It was getting late in the afternoon of March 15 when Hunter finished. The two principal ambulances that we'd ordered had just arrived, having been driven for twelve hours straight by two of our guys. There was something about the arrival of the ambulances that brought a sense among us all that we were finally ready to get to work.

Barely an hour later, the call came in. The moment Seaspray took it, held up his hand for silence, and crouched over a pad of paper, we knew it was on.

"What's the extent of their injuries?" he asked, his voice calm and clear. I could just about hear a woman's voice on the other end. "What was their last known location? Anyone they spoke with recently? Cell phones, all have US passports?"

The call ended and Seaspray added final notes to the pad before turning to us all. "There's an American journalist, Benjamin Hall. Works for Fox News. Appears the rest of his team were killed. He's severely wounded, and with his injuries possibly only has forty-eight hours to live. He won't get the care he needs in Ukraine and won't survive if he stays there."

He paused.

"He's likely in Kyiv, which is currently under siege by the Russians. He's an American, he's got a wife and two little girls at home, and no one's going to get him. If we don't go for him right now, he won't make it. Who wants to go?"

There were eleven people in the living room of our safe house that night. Without hesitation, every single man there, including Hunter, said yes.

Seaspray advised that we wait for one final call with a contact from one of our intelligence agencies—a guy who we'll call Rysko—but meanwhile we all started preparing. Seaspray delegated the teams: him as vehicle one team leader, me leading vehicle two. He was going to take Bo and Doc Jadick, while I'd travel with Dr. Will and one other teammate. Sean Lee would stay back to help monitor and coordinate everything, and our government friend Rysko would join him at base—or the TOC (Tactical Operations Center)—offering assistance and acting as liaison with US government support once Ben was back across the border in Poland. We had a third vehicle carrying additional supplies driven by former professional baseball player turned humanitarian Adam LaRoche. Adam had been in and out of Ukraine over the past weeks and just so happened to be in our living room at the right time to jump in.

We all did what we've done hundreds of times before when the balloon goes up and it's go-time. We packed our bags, delegated duties, prepped, checked and loaded vehicles and equipment, then planned our routes and briefed a final plan.

Less than an hour after the call, Seaspray received a second call from our government contacts. It was brief.

"Okay," he said to everyone when it was done. "We're going."

Within a minute everyone apart from Sean had loaded their bags into the vehicles. Everyone, including Hunter.

"You're coming?" I asked.

"Yeah," he said, eyes locked on mine. "I am."

I knew that look well. I wore it myself often. I backed off and went into the house one more time.

Seaspray and Bo were midconversation.

"Hunter thinks he's coming," said Seaspray.

I let out a sigh. "I know."

"We need him back here with Sean," said Seaspray. "It's going to be forty-eight hours at least, and someone's got to be awake here at all times. Plus, Hunter's the only one who knows how to run the TOC with the system he built. I trust him."

"I agree," I said. "But if I tell him, he's going to think I'm holding him back. One of you should do it."

I didn't follow Seaspray back out when he went to tell Hunter the news, but I could hear my son's response.

"Okay," he said, trying to answer with enthusiasm. "I get it. I'll do whatever's needed." It was clear that beneath the desire to be a team player, his tone was heavy with disappointment.

Yet again, for the third time in as many days, my heart was swollen with pride for my son. He was willing to do the important job that needed to be done and was prepared to put the mission above his own desires to come along.

At 10:55 p.m. nine of us in three vehicles rolled out of the TOC, leaving Hunter and Sean behind. We were going to get Ben Hall and bring him home to his family.

FOUR

RESCUING BENJAMIN HALL

MARCH 15, 2022
Poland–Ukraine Border

I t was eerily quiet at the border crossing. Hardly anyone was there. But even though it was 2:06 a.m. and no other vehicles were waiting to cross into Ukraine, it still took us an hour and a half to make it through. All three of our vehicles were thoroughly searched, the paperwork verified, and our own passports taken away to be checked. It was cold and boring, but I was grateful. Rysko had been able to put a call in and get diplomatic approval for our crossing from the Ukrainian authorities. Without it, Seaspray thought we'd have been waiting six hours.

Eventually the customs agents waved us through, though it seemed to me they were looking at us funny. Maybe they were thankful for us being there, maybe they thought we were crazy. I couldn't tell, but as the border disappeared in our rearview mirrors, I put the agents from my mind. We were now in an active combat zone, so I spent a little while looking around me. Despite the fact that Mighty Oaks had worked here before, it was my first time in Ukraine. There wasn't much to see. All the streetlights were out, and we were driving through the thick pines of the national forest. So after a mile or two of staring into the darkness, I tipped my seat back and prepared to sleep.

"What kind of psychopath drives into a war zone and goes to sleep?" asked one of my teammates.

I'd asked a similar question myself on one of my first deployments to Afghanistan in 2004. We'd been driving along the Khyber Pass to Jalalabad, crammed inside a rattling old Toyota pickup truck. Between the threat of IEDs and Taliban fighters, and the risk of the truck sliding off the impossibly narrow mountain paths and crashing into the valley below, I was terrified. Seeing a buddy of mine who was a SEAL curled up in the passenger seat, deeply asleep, I couldn't imagine ever being able to do likewise. But over the years I'd learned to sleep in all kinds of situations. Some people call it giving in to the contentment of war, which means accepting that whatever's going to happen is going to happen. The truth is, if you want to do your job well, you force yourself to rest when you can because you don't know when you will get the chance later.

We drove deeper into Ukraine, and I could feel my body and mind let go of the tension that had been building for days. As I exhaled and gave in to sleep, I thanked God for the gift of His peace.

I woke up to the feeling of the ambulance decelerating and Seaspray's voice on the radio.

"Checkpoint ahead. Looks like Ukrainian militia. Either way, remember: nonthreatening and relaxed. Show your hands and lots of smiles."

The checkpoint had been carefully constructed. The steep anti-tank barricades topped with razor wire and concrete jersey wall that lay staggered across the road created a serpentine path that slowed any approaching traffic. We turned off our headlights to make ourselves as nonthreatening as possible, giving the watching guards a clear shot at us as we zigzagged our way forward. Bright flashlights shone in our eyes. All of us kept our hands up and smiles bright.

I counted five guys on duty. Four old and one young. Three with AK-47s and two with hunting rifles. All of them looked like they enjoyed more than a few vodkas most days. None of them looked much like soldiers, and all of them were wearing a mix of civilian clothing and military jackets. Their gear was pieced together with no uniformity between them. There was not a single one of them who didn't look nervous.

We pulled up where we were directed and killed the engine. Roman was riding in the first ambulance and was serving as translator. He was already out of the vehicle, jabbering away in Ukrainian. The two guards who were questioning him stared back, hard and stone-faced, filter-less cigarettes hanging from mouths with missing teeth. The other three spread out with weapons drawn, trying to cover all our vehicles.

Seaspray was standing beside Roman, keeping his hands open and clearly visible, making sure his voice was calm as he tried to explain what we were doing. The main guards were firing a ton of questions, sometimes pausing for Roman to translate for Seaspray, sometimes not. At one point we all handed over our passports. As soon as the guy receiving them held them up and said, *"Americanski!"* the rest of the guards tensed. All five of them started gripping their weapons tighter, and the three covering the vehicles inched closer toward us. I remembered the rumors about Russian Special Forces posing as American humanitarian workers, and I tried to imagine what the Ukrainian guards were thinking.

One of the main guys started shouting at Roman, who was now starting to show signs of stress. Roman was talking over the guy, raising his voice. The more agitated he got, the more frantic the main guard became. It was a vicious circle, and the other guards were all feeding off the stress. Soon they were on high alert. As they moved in closer to the vehicles, I thought about what a legit EMT operator would do in a situation like this and did my best impression of someone projecting total bewilderment, as if this was the last kind of thing I'd ever expected to happen.

I've been held at gunpoint at checkpoints many times in my life. I've never liked having a gun pointed at me, and it's not good to feel out of control in a situation where people are tense and armed, but checkpoints are a necessary part of the job. If you're going to visit the kind of areas where we work, you have to learn how to talk your way out of situations like the one we were facing. I was confident that we could calm the guards down, but all the same I was relieved that Hunter was back in Krakow. I wondered how differently I'd have been feeling if he were there with us.

I watched the guards carefully. I've met killers in my life before—guys who will happily end another person's life without a care in the world. They thrive on power and get off on the rush of authority. But these guards were not like that. They were just regular men who wanted to keep their homesteads and families safe, and they were scared. We were compliant and docile, willingly submitting to their authority. All that mattered was that we demonstrated we were not a threat and didn't do anything to scare or provoke them. Soon enough they started to relax a little, and their shouting and gun waving died down.

They were still firing questions at Roman, but he was calmer, too, and Seaspray's translated banter seemed to put them at ease. The guards thoroughly searched both ambulances and asked a ton more questions about our supplies. We offered them some good tourniquets, which they happily accepted, and then they made some phone calls and waited for a response. It was a long and cold wait, but eventually we were free to go.

As we drove on, I checked my watch. We had spent over an hour at the checkpoint. With potentially dozens more ahead of us on the way to Kyiv, if they all took even half as long, by the time we arrived to rescue Ben Hall, he might already be dead.

Seaspray's voice came back on the radio.

"I've told Roman to stay quiet at the next checkpoint we reach. If we can't communicate, they can't prolong us by asking questions and will get frustrated and move us along."

He was right. Just a few miles down the road we reached another checkpoint on the outskirts of a large town. The guards manning it were just as nervous at first, but with Roman keeping silent, we were able to do our best impressions of happy, well-meaning, innocent medical-aid workers. This time there was no need to get out of the vehicles. But it still took longer than we liked. The clock was against us.

In between stops we kept in constant communication with Hunter, Sean, and Rysko back in Krakow. Rysko was able to provide real-time battlefield intelligence to guide us along a route that was, to the best of his knowledge, free from Russian forces. But in a situation so fluid and chaotic it was impossible to be sure. Since time was against us, we sped up whenever we could and ran the blue light all the time. It made us more of a target for the Russians, but there was no other choice. The clock was ticking with Ben Hall's life-threatening injuries, and for days we'd been hearing rumors that the Ukrainian authorities were considering imposing a nighttime curfew on Kyiv. As we drove, details came in: the curfew would last for at least three nights, and troops were being told to shoot on sight anyone who broke it.

It was light when we finally approached a small town on the outskirts of Kyiv. It had taken us fifteen hours to get there. We'd gone through dozens of checkpoints and made a ton of detours to avoid roads that had been bombed out. I was grateful that most of the ride had been uneventful, and I'd slept whenever I wasn't either driving or having to get through a checkpoint.

We cut the blue lights when we entered the town and received the latest report from Rysko. It wasn't good news. Russia was continuing a full press to take Kyiv, its troops already wreaking havoc in the nearby towns of Irpin and Bucha. In the distance we could see smoke rising from multiple locations and hear the sound of air raid sirens.

Our destination was a safe house nestled in the center of the town.

It was owned by a pastor we'd heard about when we visited the church leaders' meeting in Krakow a few days earlier. We knew nothing about him—just that he was alone in his house and was willing to host us for as long as we needed.

Even though the curfew was not due to start until that night, the streets were already empty. Nobody was out walking, driving, or even in their front yard. It was a ghost town. I was focused on every detail, trying to take it all in, mesmerized at the sight of a First World country in such an apocalyptic state.

The closer we got to the safe house, the more we saw. Random buildings reduced to rubble. Roads pockmarked with bomb craters. Bridges wiped out. Some of the damage was so recent that smoke was still rising from the fires within.

When we finally arrived at our destination, we went over the plan one last time. Seaspray, Bo, Doc Jadick, and Roman were to go ahead to the military hospital where Ben Hall was. That left my team plus Adam to fill the role of QRF (Quick Reaction Force), ready to go if something happened. We didn't talk long, but in just those few minutes we heard plenty of heavy ordnance exploding to the east and then the sirens cranking up again. Most of us had years of combat experience and were listening closely, trying to figure out if we were hearing Russian or Ukrainian IDF (Indirect Fire). There was no need to say anything, but we all noticed the explosions.

When we were done planning, Seaspray led his team off and I went inside, searching for our host.

Pastor Bohdan was one of those guys with an infectious smile and an ability to radiate joy nonstop. I couldn't imagine him ever being down or somber, and from the moment we said hello he was totally hospitable. He spoke English with a thick Ukrainian accent and had a ton of questions for us about what we were doing in Ukraine. I was more concerned that we got down to our tasks as the QRF. We needed to set up comms, check back in with the TOC, and—naturally—sleep.

"Sure," said Bohdan when I asked him if we could pick a room to use. "Got a basement for you."

I've never been a fan of basements at the best of times, much less in combat, and I like them even less when there are bombs actively dropping. The thought of getting buried under rubble has never been appealing, and being in a gunfight against guys above ground is a major disadvantage. As Brad Pitt's character says in the Quentin Tarantino movie *Inglorious Basterds*, "Never fight in a basement."

I chose a bedroom instead.

Judging by the décor it belonged to his daughter, who was likely about nine or ten years old. There were all the usual things you'd expect in a girl's room—soft toys and posters of cute animals—but what caught my eye was a picture on the wall, drawn in crayon. It was a classic kid's depiction of her family, all bright primary colors. But there was darkness in it as well, with heavy black bombs falling from the sky.

As I stared at it, I was transported back home to the pictures that I'd received from the children trapped in Afghanistan. Those pleading messages to Uncle Chad had tugged at my heart, and I felt the same way now. I wanted to do everything I could to help these poor children. They had been subjected to such senseless brutalities, and they didn't deserve any of it.

All day we took turns monitoring the radio and sleeping. It was mostly uneventful, and I appreciated the opportunity to check in with Hunter. If he resented being told to stay back, he didn't show it. He was executing his tasks perfectly, keeping everyone informed and updated.

I also took the chance to hand over one of our comms packages that I'd grabbed before we'd left Krakow. When there was a quiet moment, I told Pastor Bohdan I had a gift for him. He watched carefully as I unpacked the comms equipment, GPS, solar panels, and power station. He had limited understanding of this kind of tech, and I wasn't able to explain every single aspect of how it all worked, but Hunter had done such a great job putting the sets together with instruction packs that we were able to get it all set up easily enough.

When it was finally working, Pastor Bohdan got excited.

"I can see it now," he said. "We have teams all over and I can't keep track of them or reach them most of the time. Everything is happening so fast it's chaos. But now we can link everyone together on here to support each other and coordinate our efforts."

All along we'd been working on hunches and assumptions, running with the idea that these comms packages were what was needed in Ukraine. Pastor Bohdan's positive reaction was powerful and deeply encouraging. We were on the right track. Thousands of lives would be saved as a result.

———

While things were going well at the safe house, Seaspray's team had encountered some challenges. First, the checkpoints getting into the city had become a lot more frequent and the guys manning them a lot more paranoid. That had slowed the journey down a lot and heaped even more pressure on them. As they navigated their way to the medical facility, they were getting uncomfortably close to incoming Russian ordnance, and for the first time the risk of being taken out by the Russians was about even with the risk of being shot by some guy with an itchy trigger finger at a checkpoint. Then the ambulance had developed engine problems. I wasn't clear on what had happened exactly, but they were able to travel at a speed of only fifteen miles per hour. As soon as I heard this, I made sure my team was ready to roll out at any moment. "Okay, stand by," said Seaspray as the daylight faded. "We'll try and reach the hospital now. But be ready to move."

We all waited in silence in the kitchen of the safe house. Our boots were on and laced, our jackets on our backs and our bags ready to grab and go.

We waited.

Silence.

It took two hours before Seaspray's voice came back on the radio.

"We made it. And we located Ben. He doesn't look good."

The curfew began that night, but there had been a nighttime blackout in force for days. So even before dusk settled, Bohdan went around the house making sure no lights were on and all the curtains and blinds were drawn.

It was eerie sitting there in the darkness. Even more so when the air raid siren started up and the sounds of bombing intensified. The explosions hadn't stopped all day, but they'd been distant. Now they were getting closer.

It had been approximately three weeks since Putin's troops invaded Ukraine from the east, and the predicted lightning-swift victory had failed to materialize. But now, as the sound of artillery, tank shells, and missiles filled the air and shook the windows, it was clear that the Russians had not given up. They wanted Kyiv. From the sound of their attack, they wanted it now.

We waited while Seaspray's team was assessing the extent of Ben's injuries and trying to figure out a way to get him out of the city and back across the border to Poland. From everything I'd heard about Ben's condition—the open head wounds, the eye injury, the burns, the catastrophic damage to his legs and feet and left hand, and the large pieces of shrapnel lodged in his neck—there was no guarantee he would survive in the hospital, and the odds were against them even making it out of the city, let alone all the way back to safety. But the hospital was not equipped to save Ben, nor was he a priority with the mass casualties and triage protocols in place. They didn't even have pain medication for him: he was on drip ibuprofen. Moving him was the only option.

Our team was itching to go, but to be a ready QRF all we could do on our end was wait. I had to force the rest of the team to get some sleep so they would be ready to roll if we had to move, and I sat with Bohdan in the darkness of his daughter's bedroom while the night outside was filled with sirens and sounds of explosions and occasional flashes of light.

"How come you're here, Pastor?" I asked.

"It's quite a story," he sighed. For once he wasn't so full of joy and energy. "You wanna hear it?"

"Of course."

"I was working in the US for a long time. I got citizenship and all that, but about thirteen years ago I came back here. I didn't really know why, but it felt like the right thing. And ever since then, something crazy's been going on with my life. Ever since I came back, I've been meeting all these super influential people. I'm talking government leaders and military generals, some of the most powerful guys in Ukraine. And I'm just this pastor, right? I couldn't figure it out why I was meeting these people. But I also knew that I didn't have to understand fully why it was happening. I knew it had to be a God thing. I just had to go with it."

A large explosion nearby made him pause for a moment.

"When everything started happening here, I was back in the US on vacation. I still didn't understand what all those relationships were for, but I knew I needed to come back home immediately. So, while plenty of people were flying out, I flew home. I wasn't alone, though. Thousands have done the same and returned to fight."

"You could have stayed in America?"

"Legally? Yes. Personally? There was no way I wasn't going to come home. I had to be here. And almost as soon as I arrived, I understood why God had been orchestrating all those relationships. I was able to be a kind of bridge between the government and military on one side and the church on the other. Both parties know me and trust me, and because of that it's been possible for the church to step up and do all it's doing. It's crazy, right? Sometimes when I think about it I just have to laugh."

"And what do you think is going to happen?"

His tone shifted. The laughter was gone. He was serious again.

"They will never win. The Russians would have to kill every single Ukrainian to be able to declare victory. And remember, they have already been killing us for years. We're not afraid of a fight, and we're not backing down. And the Russians know that. Their morale is low, and we're hearing reports that some of their troops are choosing to run away instead of fighting us. They'd rather be in jail than die here."

Asking Russian citizens to invade Ukraine was like asking Americans to invade Canada. While Ukraine is no longer part of the Soviet Union, to millions of Russians and Ukrainians it felt like Putin was pitting neighbors against each other in a civil war.

Ben Hall had lost his legs in the attack, his eye and hand injuries were serious, and he had suffered significant burns, but the main problem was the shrapnel in his neck. Doc Jadick said that there was a risk of it coming loose and severing an artery. That made driving potentially fatal given the bombed-out state of the roads around Kyiv. Not to mention the fact that Ben didn't have the twenty-plus hours it had taken us to drive from the border in the first place. The only options were air or rail, and neither of those were actually feasible. Flying was out of the question unless you wanted to be immediately shot down, and the chances of any trains running in the middle of a war zone were practically zero.

All through the night Seaspray, Sarah, Rysko, and I had been contacting people to find a solution. After hours of getting nowhere, a possibility emerged. We learned that a secret meeting was taking place in Kyiv between the prime ministers of Poland, the Czech Republic, and Slovenia, who had come for high-level security talks with President Zelensky. They'd traveled in by train, accompanied by Polish GROM forces—their equivalent to the US Delta Force—and were due to leave that morning.

As soon as we heard about the train, we got to work trying to secure permission for Ben and the team to be on it. It was kind of frantic and relied on a bunch of things happening that were way beyond our control. We needed God to be in the director's chair, just like He'd been with Bohdan for all those years.

At the same time as we were sending up prayers and making contact with anyone who could help, we were receiving reports that updated us on the Russian attack. None of the news was good. All that shelling in the night had allowed them to make significant gains, and they now occupied a band of land just outside the city that spread from the northwest to the southeast. They were squeezing like a python, advancing ever closer toward the center of the city while trying to close the gap and have Kyiv completely encircled. A few more successful skirmishes and they'd have the city surrounded with our team trapped inside.

Eventually we had good news. Kind of. Ben and the team had been granted permission to ride on the train, but they had only thirty minutes to get to the station. It was a high-risk journey, requiring them to not only navigate checkpoints where soldiers were operating under the shoot-on-sight order but also avoid the advancing Russians—all while keeping Ben Hall alive. And they had to do it all in an ambulance that still could not go faster than fifteen miles per hour.

While the medical staff at the hospital was arguing among themselves about whether to allow Ben to leave, Seaspray did what was necessary: he took advantage of the chaos and snuck Ben out.

As Seaspray attempted the impossible, I made a quick call to Kathy. I'd been blocking the sirens out for most of the night, but she heard them right away. Instead of stressing out, she did what she always does when I call from a hot zone and started joking around.

"What's going on? I hear sirens. You going to stay inside and sit around or go out and do something to help?"

"Easy, we're going," I said. "Okay, I have to go. I love you."

"I love you too."

Finally it was time to say goodbye to Bohdan.

"I want to tell you a secret," he said as we climbed into the ambulance. "Don't follow the street signs."

"Why?"

"We spray-painted most of them out, but the ones that we didn't spray won't help you. They've likely been moved and are designed to either send the Russians in circles or direct them to an ambush point where we kill them."

I thanked him for the advice and jumped in the ambulance.

"And one more thing," he added. "I'm hearing that the government is locking the city down today. If you don't make it out now, you'll be here for a long time."

We kept in constant radio contact with the other team as well as the TOC, monitoring every movement over the radio. Things got particularly tense when Seaspray's team was ordered out of their vehicle at gunpoint at a Ukrainian checkpoint. The soldiers even pulled back Ben's bandages where his legs had been blown off just to make sure it was legitimate. They let them pass after that, and somehow Seaspray and the others made it onto the train with Ben alive. It was an incredible achievement, possible only by the grace of God and the commitment of our team.

As they rolled toward the Polish border, our team trailed by vehicle. We were ready to move in with the second ambulance if anything happened with the train, but I prayed to God that it wouldn't come to that. The train was the best option for Ben to survive the trip to Poland.

The drive to the border was long, covered with the suspense of the team getting Ben across the border safely—alive. We were just approaching Lviv when Seaspray finally radioed to confirm that they had made it. The US military had to stage on the Polish side of the border due to not being allowed to cross into Ukraine, but as soon as Ben crossed he had been loaded onto a waiting Black Hawk for transfer by the 82nd Airborne. After that he'd be taken to an aeromedical unit on standby, then on to the US Army's Regional Medical Center in Landstuhl, Germany. Ben got the same level of treatment any of our servicemembers would have received with a combat injury. He was in good hands. We all exhaled in relief.

Soon after Seaspray's message, we heard from the TOC with an update on the Russian assault on Kyiv. They had yet to gain complete control of the city, but their python grip had tightened. In the hours since we'd left they had captured more land to the south and west, including one significant building—a hospital—in the same neighborhood as the facility Seaspray had found Ben in. The Russians were holding five hundred patients and staff hostage.

GETTING PIERRE HOME

Seaspray's group had been back for a few hours by the time my team and I pulled up at the center. As I hugged Hunter, I allowed myself a silent prayer of gratitude that we had all made it back. Then there were the usual smiles and nods of approval, then on to a little light-hearted mocking about whose fault it was that the first ambulance turned out to be a lemon and had to be abandoned in Kyiv.

I was pleased to get the update that Ben Hall was alive and in surgery, but the mission wasn't over. Four others had been killed in the attack: Pierre, Ben's cameraman, and Sasha, Fox's Ukrainian correspondent, as well as two Ukrainian soldiers who were their security. I'd been thinking about all of them during the drive back. I guess we all had.

"Do we know anything about the other bodies?" I asked. "Are they recoverable?"

Seaspray shook his head. "Not Sasha. All they could find of her was a piece of her arm. Pierre was hit by shrapnel that severed his femoral artery. So, yes, there's a body, and Fox wants us to go get him out. But . . ."

Nobody needed to articulate the risk. Even in the forty-eight hours we'd been in Ukraine rescuing Ben, the Russian offensive had increased, with rockets reaching as far west as Lviv, less than fifty miles from the Polish border. Even without the increased danger, moving a dead body across an international border is insanely complicated, requiring a death certificate, an autopsy report, and a hazardous materials report. The challenge of getting Ben Hall on the train in Kyiv was nothing compared to the difficulty of wading through all that bureaucracy while the country was at war.

As we discussed it all, my mind was wandering. I thought about Sasha and her family in Ukraine as they mourned her tragic death. I thought about Pierre's loved ones, too, how desperate they would be to bring his body home. My mind flicked back to all those we couldn't get out from Afghanistan and the heaviness I'd felt knowing that I could have done more to help them.

The more we talked about heading all the way back to Kyiv and getting Pierre's body, the clearer it became that the risk was too great. It was the correct decision, but it felt like unfinished business.

Then we got the call.

It was from Jennifer Griffin, Fox News' national security correspondent at the Pentagon. She told us that Fox executives were in Poland and that they were determined to get Pierre's body back.

Seaspray ran through the reasons why it was so logistically difficult, but Jennifer didn't give in so easily. She told us that she was going to set up a call with the Fox team in Poland.

Minutes later we were all gathered around Seaspray's phone, listening to some unexpected news.

"Pierre's body's not in Kyiv. Two of our guys have brought him to Lviv. They're both Americans who work for Fox, they're scared, and they want to get out."

We all looked at each other. Getting to Lviv and back was certainly much less of a risk than going all the way to Kyiv. But the guys on the other end of the call weren't done.

"And we have Pierre's wife with us. She's here now. I'm putting her on . . ."

We sat in silence and listened to the muffled sounds of the phone being handed over.

"Hello? This is Michelle. I want my husband's body back. Can you help? Please?"

When the call ended, we talked briefly, but not about whether we should go. We talked about how we could make it work and what influence we could use to get the paperwork done so that Michelle could take her husband home.

Fifteen minutes later, at 7:50 p.m., Seaspray, Bo, and I were back in the ambulance. Thanks to Rysko, we were confident that we could get the required paperwork in time, so we headed directly to the border.

It took two and a half hours to reach it and another hour to get through. The crossing was practically deserted, but just as we were about to start driving away, a young woman stepped out from the side of the road and waved us down.

She was carrying a shoulder bag and looked more like she was out for a day of shopping than traveling into a war zone. It also didn't look like she was at the end of a journey: she looked worn out but determined, ready for the long haul to come.

Bo was driving and buzzed down the window. The woman didn't say anything at first. Just looked at each of us in turn.

"Hey," said Bo.

"American?" she said.

"Yeah. Do you need help?"

"My husband . . . fighting," she said, nodding ahead to the darkness beyond as she searched for the words. "My kids are safety. I go back now. You help me?"

"Where are you going?" Bo asked.

"Varash. North."

"I'm sorry. We're heading south."

She barely skipped a beat. Something told me that she was used to having to adapt. "Is okay. Take me short way. Please."

76

I was in the back, so I opened the door and let her in. She nodded and mumbled her thanks, but as we drove off she tensed, eyes constantly flicking between the three of us and the road. I guess she was starting to think that getting into an ambulance at midnight with three random Americans wasn't such a good idea after all. Maybe she'd heard about the Russian death squads posing as American humanitarian workers, or maybe just being a vulnerable woman alone with three strange men in a war zone was uncomfortable enough. I tried to put her at ease by offering her some of the snacks we'd brought with us and trying to talk to her about how cold it was outside. She spoke as much English as I did Ukrainian, but she happily took my yogurt pack and then dug through her bag, pulling out some cookies for me. I tried not to accept, knowing she'd need it more than me, but she was adamant, and I could tell the trade meant a lot to her.

When we'd been driving for a few minutes, Bo stopped at a junction. He turned back and told her that this was where we were heading south. There was nothing but forest all around. Out beyond the glow of the headlights was only yawning darkness.

"Good," she said, sounding almost relieved. She jumped out, waved thanks, and slung her bag over her shoulder before striding off into the frigid night. We all watched her for a few moments. Once the darkness had swallowed her whole, we turned right and carried on.

Our destination was close, and as soon as we pulled into the parking lot I saw a hearse with a driver waiting beside it. It was a pristine vehicle—black as a beetle, shiny and immaculate—nothing like the kind you'd expect to be bringing a body off a battlefield. The driver looked young and nervous, the kind of wiry guy who was ready to run at a moment's notice. Not at all like an undertaker.

The guys from Fox News were there too—correspondents Trey Yingst and David "Dudi" Gamliel, along with a security team member. We all shook hands and talked a while. The journey from Kyiv had clearly been difficult, and Trey and Dudi were exhausted and ready to get across the border. They were brokenhearted too. Pierre had been with Fox News for twenty-five years and was loved and respected by everyone. In a world that continually seems to me to be more and more selfish, I was proud to see his colleagues take the time and effort to ensure Pierre was not left behind.

My task was making sure the body in the casket was really Pierre, so I went over to the driver.

"Can I see the body, please?" I asked, looking at the coffin in the back.

"Of course, friend," he said, sounding smooth and confident, hurrying like he was angling for a tip. His manner was not at all in keeping with how wiry and edgy he looked. "Whatever you need. I'm here to help."

I was pretty sure that I knew what he wanted—and it wasn't cash. My guess was that skinny man hoped that driving a hearse would be his ticket out of Ukraine and away from the requirement that all males between the ages of eighteen and sixty be available to fight.

I'd never seen Pierre in person, but as we'd driven over the border I'd found some photographs online. He had the kind of face that made me think I'd have liked him—kind eyes creased from smiling and an epic mustache. When the driver and I lifted the casket open, Pierre was easily recognizable. I was glad that he'd been cleaned up. Whoever had placed him in the coffin had treated him with care and dignity.

I paused for a moment.

It was the driver who filled the silence.

"He's American, no?"

"No, Irish," I said, keeping my eyes locked and my voice low. Pierre was a stranger to me, but I've been around enough fallen warriors to recognize the moment that calls for quiet and respect when you're standing beside a coffin.

"And you're taking the body back to Poland?"

I pretended not to hear him.

"Listen," he said, moving closer to me and dropping his voice to a whisper. "I want to get out of here. How about I drive for you?"

I looked at him, studying his eyes. He was scared, and I didn't judge him for his fear. But he had a choice to make and a duty as a citizen. Running away wasn't going to work out well for him.

"You're an adult male," I said, moving a little away from the hearse. "They're not letting you out of the country. And besides, your job is to stay here and defend your country. We can take him home to his family."

For a while he had nothing to say, but the silence didn't last long. As his eyes flicked between his hearse and our ambulance, he spoke up.

"You're taking body?"

"Yeah."

"And the Americans?"

"That's right."

"And you've just got that one ambulance? Have you seen all their supplies? You need me to drive you."

I'd been too busy looking at the casket to notice the rest of the hearse, but as I looked I saw it was full of backpacks and rigid cases—the kind of stuff that you'd expect a couple of TV correspondents and their security guy to have with them. The skinny guy was right—there was no way it would all fit in the ambulance.

But while I agreed with him about the problem, I had a different solution.

"How much for your hearse?"

He looked at me, half confused, half upset. "No. Let me drive you."

I shook my head. His charm vanished. His whole body tensed. "The hearse is not for sale."

"It is tonight."

He paused. I could see him weighing up his options.

I interrupted his thoughts. "Listen, either you're going to make the best deal of your life right now and sell us this hearse, or we're taking it from you."

I saw Seaspray approaching with his phone up to his ear. He was on with a Fox executive and he handed the phone over to the driver and doubled down on my position by telling the driver to make himself a good deal.

While the negotiations were taking place, I sat in the driver's seat just in case the guy decided to bail and take Pierre's body with him. I looked back and saw there was a flag that had been wedged down the side of the casket—a gesture of kindness from one of Pierre's colleagues. It was the green, white, and orange of the Irish tricolor. My mind took me back to all the times I'd seen coffins holding the bodies of fallen American service-members at an airbase waiting to be sent home to their loved ones. There would always be a flag over the casket, with the stars over the head and the stripes running down toward their feet. It was always precise, always pristine—a final act as they departed the battlefield to show that their service had been valued, that their sacrifice was honored by a grateful nation.

My thoughts were interrupted by the driver returning Seaspray's phone to me. He'd been talking for only a few minutes, but judging by the size of the smile on his face, he'd gotten exactly what he wanted and just made the best deal of his life. He handed me the keys to the hearse and I got on my phone and searched for images of the Irish flag to learn the correct color pattern. I ran back to the ambulance to grab tape to arrange and affix the flag.

I climbed into the back of the hearse and set to work taping and retaping the flag onto Pierre's casket. I wanted to get it perfect, and soon lost all sense of time.

"Are you okay, bro?" Seaspray was looking at me from the back and could see that I felt overwhelmed and possibly a little erratic.

"Yeah, I'm good. I just want to get it right."

"Let me help." He climbed in the back with me and together we got the flag arranged just right: orange over Pierre's head, then white and green towards his feet. Only when it was perfect could we go.

Seaspray and I walked back to Bo, Trey, Dudi, and the security guy. They were all ready to get home. As they loaded their gear into the ambulance, Trey asked if we were the ones who had been in Afghanistan the previous summer, helping evacuate all those people.

"Yes," we said.

"We were there too," said Trey. "And Pierre. We all were."

At first I'd felt a sense of duty to respond to his wife's request for help. Now I felt connected to him. Getting Pierre home to his loved ones was a mission I completely committed to.

⸺

Seaspray and Bo took the others in the ambulance, leaving me to take the lead and drive the hearse. From the moment I'd opened the casket and seen Pierre's face, I'd felt the full weight of duty to get his body back to Michelle. As we departed from Ukraine, that feeling only grew stronger.

It was 3:30 a.m. when we crossed into Poland, ready to face the biggest challenge of all. Miraculously—thanks to the work of Seaspray and Rysko, as well as a ton of other events that I can only attribute to God—all the paperwork was approved and we were waved through.

Once we were in Poland we immediately linked up with the Fox

News executives, who were waiting for us on the highway. They had Michelle with them but didn't want her to be reunited with her husband's body at some random truck stop near the border. We followed them as they drove to a funeral home they'd made arrangements with just south of Krakow. They drove a lot faster than I'd been driving back in Ukraine, and as we topped 80 miles per hour, the old hearse started rattling and groaning, swaying from side to side. I prayed that the engine would hold out and that the brakes and steering were stronger than they felt.

In a way I was grateful for the adrenaline, since I hadn't slept more than a few hours in the previous seventy-two hours and there were two and a half hours to go until we reached Krakow. Seaspray kept in radio contact, which also helped, and I even spoke aloud to Pierre a few times, letting him know that he was on his way home.

When we finally arrived at the funeral home we met Michelle and all paid our condolences.

"Can we carry him in for you?" Bo asked.

She nodded and watched while Bo, Seaspray, and I, plus Pierre's colleagues, quietly took the casket out of the hearse and carried him inside. There was no priest present, no flowers or music, but it felt like a funeral. It was a time to grieve and a time to give thanks for the life that Pierre had lived. When we set him down inside the funeral home there was a moment of silence. I prayed for Pierre, his friends, family, and Michelle's heart, and I thanked God for the opportunity to help bring dignity to Pierre's return home, even in the smallest way.

When we were done we wanted to give Michelle and the Fox team their space, so we quickly said goodbye. Michelle hugged each of us.

"Thanks for bringing my husband back to me," she said.

We didn't tell her that we'd been against it at first, that the risk had seemed too great when the call first came in. But I was glad that we hadn't gone with our first instincts, glad that we'd gotten back into the ambulance and crossed the border again. Bringing Pierre back was the right thing to do, not just because leaving him there would have likely meant he was cremated, lost in the chaos, or buried in a mass grave somewhere. I'd not really spent much time thinking about journalists before then, but the previous four days had made clear to me the parallels between what Ben and Pierre did and a life of military service: both face risks for the sake of freedom and truth. Bringing Pierre Zakrzewski back home was a way of honoring that work and sacrifice.

By the time we made it back to the TOC it was midmorning. I was tired and ready to sleep, but seeing Hunter gave me such a boost. He was clearly happy, not just to see me but with the work he'd done through both missions into Ukraine. He and Sean had taken turns being awake, monitoring and facilitating our movement through the night. It hadn't been easy, and Hunter had needed to figure out a ton of stuff along the way, but he'd done it and was continuing to prove his worth on the team.

A lot of people look at those of us with a special operations background and assume that we've been extensively trained in every single possible thing and can approach any problem with a ready-made set of solutions that we've previously drilled and refined. The truth is way different. Most of the time when we encounter a new problem we're just as clueless as anyone. But our training kicks in through our attitude and perspective: we've been taught how to maintain composure and figure out any problem in even the worst possible circumstances.

Whether it's getting thousands of people past Taliban checkpoints, transporting an injured civilian with chunks of shrapnel in his neck out of a war zone, or moving the body of a cameraman back to his wife, there's no manual to reach for. There's just a solution waiting to be found. What makes special operations special is not the adrenaline rush of a nighttime HALO jump at zero-dark-thirty or the explosions and gunfights you see in the movies. It's the ability to stay calm under extreme pressure and be a problem solver.

Everyone on the team had been living up to that description over the past few weeks, and Hunter was no exception. He'd kept his composure right from the start, working seamlessly with Sean as they tag-teamed to keep the TOC operational 24-7. And even when Rysko, our high-level government intelligence operator, showed up at the center and spent the rest of the mission sitting beside Hunter at his desk, feeding him information and acting as liaison between our operation and the government, my son hadn't skipped a beat. He'd stayed calm when he'd seen the Russian forces closing in around Kyiv, edging closer to our team's position. He'd been able to think clearly throughout the challenge of getting Ben Hall onto the train, coordinating perfectly with Polish Special Forces and the US military. Over the course of those few days, Hunter had worked with Rysko to coordinate with the offices of prime ministers and multiple intelligence agencies as well as the 82nd Airborne. He'd stepped up so effectively that he was now an essential asset to our team.

And all along Hunter had done this while trying to operate a comms system that had been thrown together just a few days earlier. Not only that but he'd been working to improve it as well, and by the time I got back to the TOC after we'd returned Pierre's body to Michelle, he had a whole plan figured out.

"We need more stuff," he said.

"Yeah?" I didn't disagree, but the way I saw it we had yet to distribute the comms packages that he'd already assembled. "How come?"

"Our comms packages are good, but they cover only a small area. I want to set up multiple comms packages and maximize the network.

That way, if the Russians take out the cell network, we'll be covered. And even if they don't, we'll effectively have our own private comms network that we can share with the NGOs and churches."

I could understand what he was talking about, but I needed to know how much and how effective it would be.

"About $200,000."

"And that would cover how big an area?"

"Ukraine?"

"Yeah. How much of the country would it cover?"

"All of it," said Hunter, pulling up a map of Ukraine with what looked like a series of spider webs covering everything. "That's what I'm saying. We could cover the whole of the country like this. All we'd need to do is get in there and find about thirty trusted Ukrainians that we could give the packages to. That's all."

I had to pause to take it all in. Eventually, when I'd done enough staring at the screen, I reached my conclusion. "This is a big deal, Hunter."

"I know. We talked about doing something similar in parts of Afghan, but I don't think it's ever been done before."

"No," I said. "It's a big deal for the people. This is Dunkirk-level stuff we're talking about, the kind of thing that will save thousands of lives. It'll keep the NGOs and the Ukrainians in contact and make sure their comms are secure."

Hunter just grinned.

"I'm super proud of you. Good job, man."

Later that day we had a visitor to the center—Ken Isaacs. As the head of operations globally for Samaritan's Purse, Ken's seen everything, from wars to famines and natural disasters, and has sat with presidents and prime ministers, kings and dictators. Ken's the kind of guy who gets things done on a colossal scale, and he hears a lot of people telling him a lot of things about how their product or plan is going to change the world. As a result, he can instantly tell when people are out of their depth.

He was visiting to take a couple of the comms packages that Hunter had built. We all said a few words but mainly left it to Hunter to talk through the details, explaining how they'd worked on the missions into Ukraine so far and showing how everything could be tracked in real time on his computer screens.

Seaspray, Bo, and I stood and watched as Ken took Hunter's brief in.

Then Hunter moved on to the comms network he'd been telling me about. He talked about the comms packages and covering the whole country and how it wouldn't cost much more than $200,000.

When he was finished, Ken paused.

I watched and waited.

"This is incredible," Ken said. "Can we get in on this?"

Hunter smiled. "Of course. We're all in this together."

Later, when we'd slept and washed up and had time to debrief on Ben Hall and Pierre, Seaspray and I sat alone. The conversation wound around to Hunter.

"Can't call him FedEx anymore, can we?"

"Nope," I said.

"And I really need him here full time. That okay with you?"

"Of course," I said, feeling proud of everything that Hunter had done. "Just as long as he stays here, in Krakow. Right?"

Seaspray nodded. But we both knew it was never going to stay that way.

SIX

THE POWER OF TRUST

The days in Krakow became increasingly busy. We met with more NGOs and handed over more comms packages. We made trips across the border to do the same with church leaders who were part of the underground network that was getting supplies from the NGOs to the troops on the front lines. We coordinated the rescue of forty-seven disabled kids who had been left behind when their facility in Kyiv had closed at the start of the war, and were able to get Amber Elle—a nurse and head of family readiness with Fieldcraft Survival—to the border to bring medical supplies and provide aid and comfort to families in need.

Our operations center was awake and alert 24-7, with a steady stream of visiting NGO and government leaders to ensure constant coordination of our growing number of operations. And all along, between the operations, the planning for future missions, and the steady flow of leaders and other contacts that came our way daily, we were constantly monitoring events, asking ourselves the same question over and over: What will Russia do next?

The answer was revealing itself before our eyes.

We were contacted by a church leader about a large group of civilians who were leaving the city of Dnipro when the Russians blew out a bridge. The civilians were trapped on the eastern side of the river, and their leader sent us pictures showing the crowd of one hundred women and children hiding with nowhere to go. It was terrible, and my heart wanted to go and get them. But the truth was this was one of hundreds if not thousands of scenarios playing out all over Ukraine. NGOs and the Ukraine military were working day and night to move people. Being a rich agricultural land, Ukraine is covered with waterways. Many of its rivers are far too wide for even advanced swimmers to cross, and by blowing out bridges Russia could easily control movements of civilians fleeing west and Ukrainian military and NGOs moving east.

It was a grim reminder just how vulnerable these escape routes across the country were and why it was important for us to build infrastructure and solutions others could use to move people. We couldn't do it all ourselves—the need was too big—but we could change the environment and capabilities for everyone involved.

Around the same time the church leader was telling us about the people outside Dnipro, Seaspray was on a call with one of our senior military generals at the Pentagon.

"Bridges," he said when the call was over. "That's what we need contingencies for. If Russia starts taking them out or puts checkpoints on them, they'll have people trapped. We need a way to manage evacs without bridges."

At once the room kicked into problem-solver mode. Someone pulled up information on the main bridges in Ukraine, and together we identified the most likely targets that the Russians would go for. We looked at conditions, identified possible crossing points, and within a few minutes had all agreed on our best possible solution: boats.

Of course, we couldn't just grab any old boats. They'd need to be easily transportable to the needed river locations. They'd need to be reliable, relatively fast, stealthy, and capable of carrying a good number of people.

We decided on rubber inflatables similar to the F470 Zodiac CRRC (combat rubber raiding craft) that we used in special operations. They pack down small enough to fit in a large duffel and are constructed of closed-air cells, which means that they can take a few bullets and not sink. We agreed to buy a mixture of gas engines with extra fuel bladders and electric engines with long-lasting batteries that allow the boats to move in complete silence.

Trouble was, every sale of a vessel—even smaller rubber vessels like Zodiacs—is registered. If we went around Europe buying up a fleet and shipping them to our base in Krakow, there was a strong chance that it would be noticed. The Russians have one of the most robust intelligence agencies in the world, and agents are everywhere. Not much goes on in the world that Putin doesn't know about, so if a Russian intel analyst identified us buying vessels in Europe, our secret plan would have been blown. They would have taken a look at a map and likely reached the same conclusions we had about the best places to cross. When we showed up, they might be there waiting for us.

Our best option was to buy the boats in the US and get them shipped over privately. It was safer but a lot more expensive.

I've always believed that when you're doing what you know God has called you to do, there's no point in worrying about resources. Genesis 1:1 says, "In the beginning God created the heavens and the earth." God created everything, so the way I see it, He is sovereign and it all belongs to Him. If you need resources to do His will, He will make it happen. It's like the old ministry saying: "If it's His will, it's His bill."

God has already come through for us so many times. We've raised nearly $50 million over the past decade to serve hundreds of thousands of warriors at Mighty Oaks, and He'd provided. We'd needed tens of millions of dollars in a matter of weeks—as well as unprecedented permissions—to rescue seventeen thousand people from Afghanistan, and He'd been good for that too. The $300,000 that we'd needed for the comms packages and the other funds for the vehicles had come through easily. We had a strong network of donors and NGO partners who had all agreed to help, including Glenn Beck and his team at Mercury One. They had come through for us in the Afghanistan evacuations and had already committed to supporting us in our operations in Ukraine. I knew that if God wanted us to buy those boats it would all come together. But transporting them in a timely manner? That was a problem I was struggling to figure out. Shipping commercially was going to be too slow, as there were currently thousands of NGOs shipping to Europe to support their efforts, which had led to supplies being stuck in customs for weeks if not indefinitely. And even if we could find a way to get them out of customs quickly, there was a risk that the Russians would find out about what we were doing.

The only possible solution was to fly the boats in by private plane—and a pretty big one at that.

I know a couple of people with the means to own planes that big and the hearts to stop everything to help people in need, so I made a call to one of them—my buddy Korey Scott. He's a brother Marine, a combat veteran, and has been a huge part of Mighty Oaks over the years.

He answered my call right away.

"Hey, Bruce Wayne," I said. "How do you feel about ending World War III and saving a couple of thousand lives?"

"What do you need?"

"I need a plane. And it has to be big enough to carry a lot of supplies and fly to Eastern Europe."

"You got it."

And that was it. No need for explanations first or time to think about it and chew it over. Korey was on board. His family's Dassault Falcon 2000LXS plane was ours to use as we wished.

Hunter and I flew back to Texas soon after, me to source the boats and Hunter to buy the extra equipment he needed to continue building out the comms network. I'd been away for a month and it was good to get home to Kathy, even if just for a few days. I'd missed her, and unlike the times when I'd been deployed to Afghanistan, I actually wanted to tell her about what I'd experienced while being away.

I told her about the women and children in Krakow and at the border. I told her about Pastor Bohdan and the incredible work the church was doing. I told her about the NGOs and the scenes at the border, and the woman hitchhiker we'd picked up on the way to collect Pierre's body. Most of all, I told her about Hunter.

"I'm so proud of him," I said. "He's there with some of the finest, most qualified operators, and he's earned his place. He's not trying to prove anything either. He's just getting on with the task in front of him. And you should see what he's working on. It's incredible and beyond my ability. He could probably get rich off something like this as a contractor, but he's just going to give it away and let all these NGOs and churches use it."

The detail was new, but the truth behind it was nothing new to Kathy. She knew exactly how smart and generous Hunter was. For a lot of those years when I'd been serving overseas, she'd put the bulk of the time into raising our kids. And she'd done a heck of a job.

Sourcing the boats took a little longer than expected, but Hunter was keen to get back and start working, so he returned to Krakow ahead of me. There weren't many people back at the base when he arrived, just Sean and Kayla, who worked as an administrative assistant for us.

Soon after he returned, when Hunter was deep asleep, Kayla ran into his room around 3:00 a.m., panicking.

"Two vehicles just came through our gates and are driving in towards us!" she yelled. "I don't know who they are!"

Hunter immediately ran outside, followed by Sean.

Just like Kayla said, there were two unknown vehicles on the property. Both SUVs were dark, but all of their windows were down. Hunter could easily see that each one contained four guys. They were all talking, though Hunter wasn't sure if they were speaking Ukrainian or Russian. They were parked just inside the gate, about ten feet from the front door. All of the occupants were either studying our property or checking their phones.

Hunter walked up to the driver of the lead vehicle. "What are you doing here?"

The guy ignored Hunter and stared at his phone. Hunter leaned in and grabbed it out of his hand, quickly taking a picture of the screen with his own phone before throwing it back to the driver.

The guy yelled something in Ukrainian or Russian or whatever, but Hunter didn't bother getting into it with him. Instead, he took a few paces back and started taking photos of both the vehicles' license plates.

The eight guys must have been spooked by Hunter and Sean, and they quickly backed out of the gates and drove off. Hunter sent all the images to Rysko to see if anything came up on the vehicles, but nothing did. Wherever the guys were from, if they'd done enough planning to hack the clicker that opened our tall metal gates, they were smart enough not to leave a trail for us to follow. But the real reason for their visit wasn't hard to guess. They were sending us a message: "We're watching you." At least now they knew we weren't a soft target.

In spite of everything that was happening in Ukraine, the work of Mighty Oaks at home continued. Before heading back to Krakow, Korey and I took a trip to Camp Pendleton, California—the West Coast base of the US Marine Corps—where I had the honor of addressing the graduating class of Basic Reconnaissance Course–Class 2–22. This was my third time as a guest speaker at a BRC graduation, and while I felt the same burden to say something that these warriors would remember for a lifetime, with everything that I had seen so far in Ukraine fresh in my mind, my desire to encourage and inspire them was even greater.

"As Reconnaissance Marines and as men, you will continually be given the choice to do what is right, to do what is wrong, or to do nothing," I said in closing. "Remember this: there is never a wrong time to do the right thing. I trust when the time comes, you will follow the giants who came before you, and you will do what is right."

I ended with a BRC saying: "All it takes, is all you got."

I headed back to Krakow a couple of weeks later. Unlike Hunter, who had flown commercial with even more checked luggage than he had the first time, I flew in the luxury of Korey's pristine family jet. Tyler Merritt, founder and CEO of Nine Line Apparel—one of the largest veteran-owned apparel companies—is a great friend and humanitarian. He hitched a ride with us to engage in lifesaving work there.

It wasn't entirely stress free, though. The Falcon 2000 was his mother's pride and joy, designed for comfort and luxury, not cargo. Stuffing the jet with boats, gas and electric motors, fuel bladders, and batteries without causing damage to the interior was a challenge. I was grateful that Korey, who was coming along for the ride, was super cool about it, as was his pilot, another former Marine. All the same, I apologized for taking so long to pack the plane.

"You're kidding," said the pilot. "This is the best trip I've had since the Marines! It beats taking a bunch of rich folks to play golf."

After a short stop for fuel in Newfoundland we arrived back in Krakow on March 31. The weather had changed in the time I'd been at home, and it no longer had the same World War II foggy gloom. The sun was out and there were signs of spring all around.

There were also signs of a change in Russian tactics.

From the start we'd been aware of the rumors of the Russian kill squads going into Ukraine posing as American humanitarian workers. But as the war had entered its second month, whispers began that Russian Special Operations snipers were actively targeting genuine US humanitarian workers in Ukraine—people just like us. None of us were surprised by this, but it was something we factored in to each mission we undertook over the border.

Just before I'd landed back in Poland, the rumors were proven true: we received credible reports that Russian snipers had killed an American aid worker in Ukraine. Between this, the tracker on our car at the Sheraton, and the incident at base when Hunter had scared away the nighttime visitors, it was clear that the kind of work we were undertaking was reaching the attention of the Russians.

It didn't change the big picture. If anything, it made us more determined to continue our work to rescue those who couldn't rescue themselves and support the efforts of the NGOs and the underground church network. But I'd be lying if I said I didn't think about it, wondering, *Will I ever let Hunter go with me on a trip over the border, into Ukraine?*

I didn't have to wait long before the question was a reality. There was a church in Lviv that was a key part of the underground network that was moving supplies given by the NGOs to the troops on the front line. The church needed to be able to communicate effectively with others in the network without fear of compromise. They needed one of our comms packages, and after my unimpressive attempts to demonstrate it to Pastor Bohdan, it was clear that Hunter was the best person for the job. On top of that, making his first trip into Ukraine would allow Hunter better insight into continuing to build the comms network.

Taking Hunter was a no-brainer, but it left me feeling nervous all the same, just like the previous summer. The time had finally come that I could no longer stop the inevitable. Hunter was a combat veteran from

Afghanistan, but could I really take my own son into a war zone and treat him as my teammate? Could I let go of being his dad like that?

I prayed about it and talked to Kathy as well as others. It felt different this time.

Hunter had proved himself in Poland. Now it was time to trust that he would do the same in Ukraine.

We left the TOC on day forty-nine of the war, an almost-warm Wednesday morning in April. Driving across the border hadn't gotten any quicker since our first trip, and it took a couple of hours to have our papers, passports, and vehicle checked before we were waved through and on into the forest. For the people coming the other way, it was the same old story, and the road out of Ukraine was still a clogged artery. The line of cars was well over three miles long, and Hunter and I passed in silence. He needed to see it for himself, to absorb the scale of what was going on.

Going to Lviv was a relatively short distance on a map but a slow journey in reality. There were just as many checkpoints as before, maybe more. At every one, the same nervous hands clasping the same Russian-made AK-47s. Nothing good ever happens when nervous people holding deadly weapons get spooked.

After we'd been driving a few hours, we approached the city and found ourselves in a scene that could have been anywhere in Texas. There were gas stations and pizza restaurants and car dealerships, all selling the same global brands as back home. People were trying to go about their normal life—old ladies walking their dogs, kids playing ball, even an old guy fishing from a bridge—but the signs of war were everywhere. There were checkpoints and sandbags all around, and every soldier we saw appeared alert and on edge.

The column of black smoke up ahead told us why. As we approached, we saw that it was the aftermath of a Russian strike on a fuel depot. From the thickness of the smoke, I guessed it had happened just a day before, maybe two.

It was a brutal attack, one of the main ones to hit Lviv since the invasion had begun. By this stage in the war the Russians' use of ballistic cruise missiles had been well reported, but this was my first time seeing the aftermath of a strike with my own eyes. Two missiles, both roughly the size of a telegraph pole, had been used in this particular attack. There was nothing much left of the depot. Or the shopping mall. Or the grocery store. Or the rows of houses nearby. Nobody was searching for survivors.

Hunter drove slowly as we passed by, part out of curiosity, mostly out of respect. He was doing great. I, on the other hand, could feel the first wave of doubt. What kind of father takes his son on a road trip into a war zone?

Was Hunter ready for this? Was I?

For a big part of Hunter's childhood I was not in a good place. By the time he was thirteen years old, my life was unraveling fast. After eight special operations deployments to Afghanistan, I was deep in the pit of PTSD, and I had brought my family along with me: Hunter, his younger brother, Hayden, and their sister, Haili. And Kathy too. I'd pushed everyone away. As far as I could tell, the only option ahead of me was killing myself and becoming another veteran suicide statistic.

It seems that some of the biggest changes in life happen only when we're pushed to our limits. That's how I was molded to become a Force Recon Marine, and it's how I became a father and husband again. I was ready to give up on myself, but there were a handful of people around me who weren't. They refused to be swayed by the man I'd become, and they still had faith in the man God had created me to be. It took a lot of prayer and a lot of tears, but six months after being suicidal, my life had been transformed. Not changed. Not improved. Transformed. I was a new creation, plain and simple.

It was through these new eyes that I saw my wife and my children clearly for what felt like the first time ever. I saw their gifts, their characters, their potential. Each of them blew me away. I decided to make up for lost time and threw myself into the task. I was obsessed, reading every book about parenting that I could get my hands on. It was like I was planning for the most significant mission of my life, which I guess was exactly what I was doing.

I read *Captivating* by Stasi Eldridge to understand Kathy and Haili better as women. After reading one particular book, *Raising a Modern-Day Knight* by Robert Lewis, I got real deliberate about everything with my boys, who were becoming young men. Over several weeks and months, I followed the program that taught them what it meant to be a man of God. The whole thing culminated in a ceremony in which I got to tell Hunter and Hayden exactly what I saw in them.

"Hayden, your attention to detail isn't OCD; it's being organized and deliberate. Your work ethic and drive to make me proud will make you extremely successful at anything you put your heart, mind, and hands to."

Hunter was fourteen at the time but was old enough to be aware of what I had been through and the changes I was making in my life. He was one of the people who never gave up on me, and he has been a major catalyst in my restoration to the life I live today. Back then he needed different words than Hayden, but my conviction was just as strong.

"It's your integrity. Your character. Your leadership. Your heart for others. And you've got a spiritual resilience so solid that nothing can break it."

In the thirteen years since I hit my rock bottom, God has taught me so much. He's surrounded me with people who love and care for me enough to fight for me. He's given me mentors who have discipled me and taught me how to recalibrate my life. Most important of all has been the second chance and grace that God gives us all. It turns out that rock bottom is a pretty good foundation to rebuild your life on.

—◆—

After several hours of driving through Lviv, we were only a few miles from our destination when we saw a checkpoint ahead. We'd been through almost a half dozen already that day, and this one looked no different—the road blocked by the same collection of old tires, broken down vehicles, and sandbags, a raggedy old tent to the side doubling as a guardhouse.

Hunter slowed us to a crawl.

The three civilians staring at us all had their hands on their weapons—AK-47s, of course—their yellow and blue armbands prominent. But the clearest thing of all was their nerves. All of them looked wired and scared, their eyes darting between each other and us, their weapons trained on us as we inched closer.

I'd been through so many checkpoints by this point in the war that I'd gotten used to the routine, with big guys wanting to look tough and dominant in front of the smiling American aid workers. But right from the start it was clear that this was different. These three weren't giving off macho vibes. They were putting out authentic fear.

Hunter exhaled as he pulled to a stop. The youngest guard, a woman not much older than Hunter, approached his open window inch by inch.

"*Amerikanski,*" Hunter said.

Her reaction was instantaneous. Her eyes widened. She took a half step back, adopted a defensive posture, and clenched her AK tight. Something was definitely abnormal. She called out to one of the other guards—a heavy guy who was holding his rifle like it was a life raft. Her voice was shaky, laced with panic. He was by her side in seconds.

"Amerikanski," Hunter said again, smiling this time, slowly holding up our passports.

The big guy was even more nervous than the girl. He jabbered a couple of sentences and glanced over toward the third guy, who was clearly the boss. By the time he joined, all three of them were just about ready to snap.

The boss leaned toward the open window and tried to look inside. He pulled out his phone and opened up Google Translate.

"Where . . . you . . . go?"

Hunter pointed to the location on the phone that was stuck on the dash. "Supplies," he said. "Radios." The boss looked blank and it was Hunter's turn to search for the translation.

"Passports," said the boss. Hunter held them out the window.

"Phone," he barked.

Hunter didn't skip a beat and meekly passed it out the window too. My mind was racing, but I had to allow Hunter to take the lead. He was the one who had been driving; he was the one they wanted to talk to.

"Get out," the boss said to Hunter. "Show me . . . trunk."

We'd talked about this kind of scenario a couple of times already, and I was confident that Hunter knew the deal and that he wouldn't give anyone a reason to get any more nervous than they already were. I was the one who was struggling. If I got out of the vehicle and started interfering, it would definitely make matters worse, so my only option was to sit right where I was, stare at my phone, and play the part of a bored aid worker who had nothing to hide and no reason to be scared. But staying there, abandoning my boy to get through this whole experience on his own, was one of the toughest things I've ever been through.

As Hunter's dad, I was desperate to go and join him, or even to turn around and give him a reassuring smile. All I could do was sit, listen, and allow him to do his thing.

Hunter was doing everything we'd talked about. He sounded calm and I could hear the smile in his voice as he talked through the boxes of supplies we had with us. But he was ready and alert too. I could hear that in his voice as well.

"You want a solar charger?" he asked, turning from guard to guard, keeping everyone engaged. "These ones are really good. We've got a spare here."

The boss grunted. "I take passports," he said as he walked toward the tent. "I check."

After that, we waited. Hunter stayed at the back while the other two searched the car. The girl pulled everything out while the big guy stood to the side, his muzzle swinging back and forth between Hunter and me. I was still in the front, still staring at my phone, still trying to look calm and unbothered.

The girl finished the search but we were still waiting for the boss to return. Hunter loaded the equipment back into the trunk and waited where he'd been all along. The girl stepped back and covered Hunter with her AK. The big guy shifted his attention to me only.

Inwardly I was praying silently, but outwardly I was looking occupied on my phone. There are a lot of ways to get killed in a war zone, and I've spent most of my life learning to avoid them. But sitting in a car playing Tetris has never been the kind of death I've imagined.

Fifteen minutes passed. It felt like an hour. Hunter was out back, I was in the front, two guards stood to the side with one weapon trained on each of us. All of us waiting.

Finally the boss emerged. He was holding out the passports and Hunter's phone.

"Go."

Hunter nodded, climbed back in the car, and drove us away. Silent and slow.

Neither of us had any idea why they were so spooked, but we were happy to move on. Only when they'd disappeared from our mirrors did Hunter and I both relax just a little.

"I was watching you back there," I said.

Hunter nodded.

"You did great, buddy. You ready for what's next?"

"Always," he smiled. "This is a young man's game."

I laughed. "Not really, but you're doing good."

It was getting late in the evening when we reached our destination, a house on the outskirts of Lviv. This far west there was little to no danger of running into Russian troops, but the risk of air attacks remained, so we got down to work quickly, handing out and explaining how to use the comms kits.

We were visiting friends of Pastor Bohdan, a husband and wife who were local pastors. They looked tired, as if they'd been living off too little sleep for too many days. All the same, they were appreciative and committed to learning what Hunter had to show them. As he carefully demonstrated how to use the satellite radios, solar equipment, and tracking systems that we'd brought with us, their focus never wavered. The woman, Maria, spoke great English, and she was tireless in her work as translator. She was constantly checking with Hunter to make sure she'd understood correctly before passing the instructions on in Ukrainian to her husband. She was clearly taking it seriously, and for a moment I wondered what her life had been like before the war began.

I mainly studied Hunter as he worked. As an ANGLICO Marine he'd been in similar situations before, training others from foreign nations how to use complicated equipment—he'd trained and worked with South Koreans, Canadians, Georgians, and Afghans—but those were other military men from allied forces. They knew how to take instruction and had some knowledge already in place. This couple had likely never picked up a gun before the war, let alone received training in how to use state-of-the-art, high-tech comms equipment. They had lots of questions and got a ton of stuff wrong, but Hunter only ever responded to them with patience and kindness.

Once Hunter was finished and there were no more questions to answer, Maria insisted she feed us and that we stay the night. The food was delicious—a strip of beef and a brothy soup loaded with local vegetables—and the beds she made up for us were way more comfortable than I expected. Hunter and I woke early the next morning feeling refreshed and excited to drive farther south and deliver another set of equipment to more people who Pastor Bohdan had recommended.

We packed our gear while Maria prepared breakfast, and we came back to the kitchen to find the table set for two with steaming cups of coffee, fresh fruit, an egg each, and tasty pastries.

Her husband had already headed out for a trip, so she sat alone with us but didn't say much while we ate. She smoked a cigarette and stared at us the whole time, but her gaze was kind and not calculating or suspicious. She had this serenity about her, a half smile resting on her face. It was kind of wistful, gentle, as if she was happy to simply savor the moment, watching a couple of guys eat the breakfast she'd just prepared. It was peaceful sitting there like that, a normal, everyday act that made the stress of the war and all that she had lost fade just a little.

It was only when we drained the last of the coffee that she started to speak.

"When Pastor Bohdan told us about you, I was not sure to believe him. A lot of people make promises these days, but not everything they say actually happens. So, I am grateful that you came."

"It's our pleasure," I said. "We just want to show you that you're not alone in this."

Pastor Maria's half smile dropped. She opened her mouth to speak, but her breath caught. She fell silent. Then she swallowed back whatever emotion had been trying to battle its way to the surface and took a deep drag of her cigarette.

Over the years I've sat with many people who have been weighed down by grief and sorrow. I've felt it myself. I know what it looks like, what it feels like when it rises up. And I know that what's needed is silence and a listening ear, not easy solutions or quick changes of subject. So, I said nothing. I felt an urge to glance at Hunter, that old protective dad instinct rising up again. But I knew I didn't need to check on him. He had already proven himself this trip.

"My son," she said after a silence long enough for half the cigarette to burn away. "I want to tell you about him."

Another silence, but this time Hunter broke it.

"We'd love to hear about him."

Maria's smile flashed back. "His name was Andriy, and he had just turned nineteen in January. He was talking about studying engineering and wanted to go to university. But he was also talking about leaving Ukraine and becoming a chef on yachts owned by super rich people. Andriy was like that, always with some big, new idea in his head. And who knows, maybe he would have done them all anyway.

"When the war started, he was sent to Kharkiv. He said he was happy to go, and he wanted to fight, but I was worried for him. All his friends were into boxing and MMA and all those things like you, but not Andriy. He'd never been a fighter. Always a—what do you say? It begins with *n*."

"Nice?" Hunter suggested.

"No. A . . . nerd. That's what he called himself. A nerd. But still he was happy to fight. He said it was his duty. And so he went. He was given a gun, a few days' training, and sent to the front lines to defend the city."

Maria paused and lit another cigarette. It took a couple of long drags before she was ready to go again.

"I was not told any news about what happened. Just that there was a Russian attack and Andriy was hit by metal from the missile. It hit his leg." She pointed to the top of her thigh, right by the femoral artery. "Just here."

Another silence. Shrapnel to the femoral artery had been the cause of Pierre's death too. Both of them would have likely bled out in less than five minutes.

"I know this because one of the men who was with Andriy phoned me after he'd died. The man said that he had called for a medic, but none of them was around. He said Ukrainian soldiers are not given any real medical training or equipment, and that soldiers are told not to do first aid on each other. Only doctors can treat a wounded man, even if he is dying. So even if he had a bandage or anything like that, he could not have used it to help Andriy without knowing how. All he could do was hold him as he died."

"That doesn't make sense," I said, forgetting about listening in silence. "How can they ask people to fight and die for their country but not give them basic medical supplies and training?"

Maria shrugged. "They say you can treat yourself, but what good is that when you're dying? And nobody has the right equipment anyway."

In the first days and early weeks of the war, when the world was watching 24-7 and the news networks were chronicling every step, the story of Ukraine's resistance had surprised almost everyone. To some extent we'd all bought the same lie as Putin during the buildup, assuming that Kyiv would fall quickly and that it was all going to be over in a matter of days.

Instead of rolling over, Ukraine had done everything they could to defend their capital, creating miles and miles of barriers around it. They'd erected miles of wire and dragged city buses out to the perimeter and set them alight, stacking them in the road. It was desperate, and it had worked. Against all odds they had halted the Russians and delivered an incredible psychological blow. But that last-ditch mentality couldn't go on forever. In war, and in life in general, you can't build a winning strategy out of Hail Mary passes.

From what Maria was saying, the Ukrainian troops were being treated just like Kyiv's city buses. To send them out without a proper medical kit or the training to use it was as wasteful and desperate as using an entire city's transport network as a burned-out roadblock.

"We don't want anyone to come and fight for us," said Maria, clearing up the breakfast things. "We will stand here and fight Putin until every last one of us is dead, just like Andriy. But we do need help. We need equipment, like what you have given us, and other supplies. That is all we need—the tools to fight. We can provide the bodies. So when you go, please tell people this. Tell your leaders to do the right thing so that Ukraine's people can defend themselves."

Then she asked if we could pray together. Her prayer was simple, but it left me stunned. She didn't ask God for anything. Just listed all the things she was thankful for.

We said goodbye soon after and drove away, heading south. Hunter was driving again, and as I looked at him, I realized he was feeling exactly like me.

"You okay?" I said.

He shook his head. "I've never met pastors like that before."

"I know. Nothing about her life is comfortable. Maybe it never will be again. But she's not running away. She's risking it all. And she's finding God is right there in the fear and the risk."

Hunter nodded. There was a pause. "What she said about the troops not having med supplies or training to be able to treat each other. If that's true . . ."

A mile went by.

Finally Hunter said exactly what I'd been thinking.

"We have to do something, don't we?"

I knew the answer was yes, and I knew how we were going to do it.

As I mentioned earlier, at Mighty Oaks our message is simple but life changing. We encourage resiliency by strengthening the four key pillars in life: mental, physical, social, and spiritual. The troops in eastern Ukraine needed medical supplies to heal their bodies, but they also needed a spiritual solution for their hearts, minds, and souls. It would be our privilege to serve them with both.

SEVEN

MOVING TO KYIV

It wasn't difficult to decide to pack up our operations center in Krakow and leave Poland entirely. Hunter's encounter with the nighttime intruders had bothered us, and there were now even more Russians and foreign intelligence agencies from every corner of the globe milling about the streets and restaurants of Krakow. Three months into the war, there were times when it felt like the city was hosting an international spy convention. We'd stayed as long as we could; it was time to go.

The security situation pushed us out, but there was also a pull toward our next destination. The Ukrainian military hadn't just resisted the Russian advance on Kyiv—they had pushed the invasion way back, which meant that the city was now relatively safe and stable outside of rocket attacks. It made sense for us to be there: we would have better access to church networks, be able to make contacts within the Ukrainian military, and have a faster response time that didn't include the border delays every time we had an operation to respond to.

The decision was easy. The logistics of making the move were anything but.

In the months since I'd arrived, we'd acquired a lot of equipment: comms gear, med supplies, general stuff that a half dozen guys need to live, as well as Seaspray's vast supplies of survival stuff, the boats, and a fleet of vehicles. We had ambulances, vans, trucks, SUVs, rail trucks, and an off-road, six-wheel heavy transport vehicle. We could just about pack all our gear into the vehicles, but we didn't have enough people on team to drive them the 540 miles to Kyiv. A further problem was that the rail truck was slow, which meant it was going to take about twenty hours for our snaking convoy to complete the drive, and that wasn't factoring in checkpoint delays.

We called in some favors and added some drivers, then divided up the vehicles among us. Seaspray drove one of the ambulances, Roman took a van, Bo and Hunter were in separate SUVs, and Sean was in the six-wheeler truck. We'd also gained a new member of the team, Dennis Price—the Force Recon sniper who'd accompanied me when I'd gone into Tajikistan and Afghanistan the previous summer. Dennis got an SUV while I got the rail truck. I didn't mind so much. The thing was a beast and had a pretty comfy seat. To my mind, the lack of top speed only meant that there was less opportunity for things to go wrong.

Things went wrong quickly.

Seaspray was leading the convoy through a residential neighborhood about halfway between Lviv and Kyiv when he stopped and jumped on the radio. "Stop! The road's blown out up ahead. We gotta back up."

The road was lined with brick walls and fences marking the different property boundaries. For every other driver it wasn't a big deal. The road wasn't very wide, but it was easily big enough for a regular vehicle to reverse back and turn around. For me, in my oversized rail truck with no backup camera and zero visibility of anything close in my mirrors, it was a challenge. I concentrated hard. Took it slow. I was creeping forward a few feet with the wheel locked one way, then throwing it into reverse, hauling the wheel back the other way and edging back. It must have taken me three or four minutes, but eventually I was facing the other way and our journey could continue.

The radio had been silent while I executed my ten-point turn, and it wasn't until we started driving that I heard Seaspray's voice again.

"Too bad about those people's wall," he said.

I looked in my mirror and could see a pile of rubble where the wall had been. I felt terrible but there was no time to go back. All I could do was crack a joke to hide my embarrassment.

"Dang. War is hell."

The drama of the journey continued a couple of hours later when we stopped to refuel. We'd just paid when the attendant's phone buzzed. His face turned pale as he read the message.

"Everybody out! Hurry! Go!"

He swept us out of the store, then locked up behind him and sprinted over the forecourt and into a building whose windows were covered in sandbags.

"Uh, guys?" said Roman, holding up his phone. "I think I know what freaked the guy out. I just got an automated text warning of incoming fire in the region."

We didn't hang around either.

The rest of the drive was uneventful, until Sean came over the radio letting us know the six-wheeler had a flat.

We were in the middle of Ukrainian farming country, where sunflower fields spread out as far as you can see. It was like pulling over in the middle of West Texas, miles from anywhere, and the nearest town was at least two hours away in any direction.

We set to it, unfastening the four-foot-tall tire and searching for the tools we'd need. While the principle of jacking up and swapping out a six-wheeler tire is pretty much the same as it is on a regular car, the weight and size of these truck wheels—not to mention the trucks themselves—made our job a whole lot more difficult. Especially when we realized we didn't have all the tools that we needed to complete the job.

After a few minutes of scratching our heads, frustration started to kick in.

"Wish this had happened in a city," Sean said. "We're too far from anywhere to get any help with this."

I didn't feel quite so pessimistic. From my experience in rural countries around the world—as well as growing up in the bayou country of south Louisiana—I was sure that the bored, good old boys of central Ukraine would be out any minute to rally and help. All we needed to do was wait.

It took ten, maybe fifteen minutes before the locals started arriving. Neighborhood children came first, followed by a couple of barrel-chested dudes who looked as tough as any redneck American farm boys I'd ever encountered. When they came close and asked what was going on, Roman explained our problem. Instantly they got to work.

First, they made some calls. Soon even bigger dudes showed up. They were bare-chested, and the one with the biggest barrel chest of all took charge. He looked like a cross between a WWE heavyweight and the old-time sea captain, Skipper, from *Gilligan's Island*. He even had the skipper's hat on and was missing a bunch of fingers. He walked like a bear and had the biggest plumber's crack you've ever seen in your life. When he spoke, everyone obeyed.

The farmers got to work alongside our guys, but it was slow work. Soon, it felt like the whole village was there with us by the side of the road. There were so many kids running around—at least a dozen—as well as guys on crutches, a bunch of women laughing, and even more plumber's cracks on display from the guys crowding around the wheel. At some point someone brought out a cow on a rope, though I never did find out why. The whole thing was clearly the most exciting event to take place in a long time for the town.

When we'd been there for a few hours, Dennis left with one of the locals to get more tools. They returned with not only tools but some local moonshine and cake that was as hard as a brick. The guys started passing it around, insisting everyone have a taste of each. Everyone joined in except Seaspray.

"I've seen this movie," he said. "I don't want to wake up chained to the floor of a basement with a kidney cut out."

The whole thing was kind of wild, especially with all these kids running around. In between the laughter and the strangeness of it all, we got snatches of their story. We found out that when the war started, the kids' fathers—and some of their moms—had left to fight. Until their parents returned, the village was taking care of them.

It took almost six hours before the truck was fixed up and ready to drive again. The farmers didn't want to take any money for their time, but we insisted they at least accept $1,000 to help feed and clothe the kids in the village while their parents were away. Eventually they finally agreed. I guess there are good ol' boys everywhere you go.

———

We arrived in Kyiv later than we expected, making our way to an industrial unit on the edge of the city. Half of the warehouses were only partially constructed, and of the ones that were complete, only a handful appeared occupied. The whole place was practically deserted. It was perfect.

We were there thanks to Vitaly, a contact of Seaspray's who had previously been on President Zelensky's security detail but was now dedicating himself to two tasks in the war: (1) establishing an NGO that supported people who chose to stay in Kyiv by quickly repairing their homes when they were damaged in Russian attacks and (2) gathering fellow pastors and sending them to the front lines to minister to troops. Both Seaspray and I thought we had a like-minded agenda with Vitaly and could lock arms with him in accomplishing all of our missions.

Vitaly had told us that he had access to a vacant unit previously owned by the Ukrainian Secret Service. If we wanted it, the unit was ours. As we pulled up outside the twenty-thousand-square-foot ware-house and saw the secure perimeter fence, double-height roller doors, and no overlooking buildings, it was clear that Vitaly had come through for us.

He arrived just after we did. From the little I knew about him, his bio was varied. In addition to working on Zelensky's detail, Vitaly was an MMA fighter and Muay Thai boxer, Christian pastor, family man, and humanitarian worker. The moment he got out of his Land Cruiser it all fell into place. He was big and good-looking, with a mouth full of ice-white veneers and a hug that could crush a cow. I liked him instantly.

While a few of the guys rested up, Vitaly took out his phone and started showing Seaspray and me photos of the work he was doing with his NGO.

"We are called 'Under A Peaceful Sky,'" he said as he scrolled through before and after pictures of homes they'd fixed. The photos all had people standing in the foreground and staring at the camera, wearing almost identical expressions: anxious and weary in the before shot, then marked by joy and relief in the second alongside their home repaired by Vitaly's team.

"The weather's okay now," said Vitaly, "but if your roof or windows are damaged when winter comes, you have no choice but to leave. Most of these people have lived in their homes for decades—some all their life. To leave now makes them full of fear. By fixing their homes, we give them peace, even in the midst of war."

I listened hard. With every photo I saw and every story Vitaly told, my appreciation for what he was doing grew. I had no frame of reference for the situation—I'd never had to go away and fight and leave my loved ones in a war zone—but I could easily feel the deep gratitude that the troops fighting to defend their country must have felt for Vitaly and his team. Under A Peaceful Sky was taking timber, roofing sheets, screws, and windows, and it was turning them into beautiful demonstrations of love and care for the wives, mothers, grandmothers, and children left behind.

It was powerful to see behavior like this. I've seen plenty of people in plenty of war zones, and a lot of them are scared and choose to act out of primal instincts of self-preservation. They do what they can to find safety for themselves and their loved ones. They retreat, knowing that their survival depends on it. But not everyone's like that. Some people are like Vitaly: When the danger increases and the risks multiply, their courage rises. They look out, not in. They think of others, not themselves. Their faith makes them bold.

The next day Vitaly took Dennis and me to see some of the houses his guys were working on. He brought a couple of other pastors with him: Costa and Dimas. While Vitaly was tall, handsome, and polished like a Fortune 500 CEO, Costa and Dimas were unique in their own ways. Combined, they made a unique trio. Costa was six-four, three hundred pounds, and had the kind of face that was either smiling or about to erupt into laughter. He radiated so much infectious joy that I immediately nicknamed him "Costa Rica." He was confused at first, but once I'd explained it's a beautiful tropical vacation place, he loved the nickname.

Dimas, on the other hand, was a beast of an athlete. He was quiet and stoic in his demeanor, with practically 0 percent body fat, eyes like lumps of coal, and a handshake made of iron. A decade earlier he'd been a national and European wrestling champion and even made it onto the Ukrainian Olympic wrestling team. You couldn't have found two men more different from each other, but they had the same warmth, the same compassion, and the same courage as Vitaly. They told me that, like

Vitaly, they had been serving as chaplains since the war began, doing whatever they could to serve the troops. Riding in the car with the three of them, I could feel my faith grow stronger with every breath. These men were the real deal.

First we visited an older lady. The work on her home had only just begun, and Vitaly's crew was still clearing up from the aerial attack that could so easily have killed her.

"Look," Vitaly said as we pulled up outside a two-story brick home where builders were working on the roof. "This whole neighborhood and area for miles and miles is residential. Not a single military target in sight. Yet almost every home was damaged."

I stared long and hard, tried to imagine what justification the Russians could have had for attacking this quiet residential street. I could come up with only one answer: an evil desire to instill fear.

"Come," said Dimas, leading us inside. He, Costa Rica, and Vitaly greeted the woman who was standing in the doorway. It didn't take her long before she was crying.

I held back for a moment. The story of what had happened was easy to read. A bomb—possibly a rocket that would have been detonated overhead—had hit her roof, blowing off the roof itself, taking out all the windows, and sending shrapnel everywhere. Shards of metal in half-inch chunks were embedded in the walls and floors every ten to twenty inches. I dug a piece out with my knife to keep as a reminder.

Vitaly called me over. "She wants us to pray with her. Come. Join us."

I don't remember much of what we prayed, but I do remember the way it felt to be standing there, outside the scarred and broken home, with this woman, Dennis, and my three new brothers in Christ. In the midst of complete destruction, I felt like we were precisely where God was at work.

From there we drove to see another home where the work was

complete. On the way, Vitaly told me the name of the suburb—Bucha—and I recognized it from the news. It had been hit by cruise missiles in the first days of the war, then taken over by Russian forces in March—first with artillery, then tanks, then infantry. The Russians had occupied it for the rest of the month, setting up checkpoints, doing house-to-house searches, and murdering civilians. When Ukrainian forces had recaptured it in early April and the truth of the Russians' actions had emerged, President Biden had called Putin a war criminal.

As we drove into Bucha, what I saw was worse than I had expected, worse than the story the media had communicated. Parts of Bucha had been decimated. Whole streets were reduced to rubble. From the holes in several parked and burned-out cars, I was pretty sure the Russians had been firing 25 mm or 30 mm rounds, most likely from tanks. If the attack on the previous house had been designed to instill fear, what I saw in Bucha could have been planned with only one goal in mind: an evil intent to terrorize.

We drove down one street where the attack had been particularly severe. Vitaly pulled up outside a lot occupied by a small single-story house of brick and timber, hastily constructed among piles of rubble.

An old man emerged, greeting his three Ukrainian brothers warmly. When Vitaly asked him to explain what happened and offered to translate, he nodded somberly and began.

"He says he was sitting down to eat with his wife and grandchildren when he heard a noise," Vitaly translated. "They opened the door to look outside and saw a tank. The turret turned toward them, and they ran inside and into the basement. It fired soon after, maybe two or three times. The whole house exploded above them. Everything went black."

Vitaly paused, but the old man carried on, calmly retelling the story.

"They could hear the gunfire and fighting going on in the street. It lasted a long time, but when it was over, they tried to get out. The whole house was down, so their only chance was to get one of their grandchildren to squeeze out through a hole and then dig them out himself."

The old man was pointing to the ground nearby with one hand, reaching into his pocket with the other.

"When they finally did get out," Vitaly continued, "there was a dead Russian right here on the ground. The man wants me to tell you that he searched him and found this knife."

The old man was holding it out to me. I took it and opened it. There was some Russian writing on it, and the blade was about as long as my finger. It was good and sharp. I smiled, nodded, and handed it back.

"No," said Vitaly. "He says he used it to take out the Russian's teeth. He says that he's keeping the teeth but that he wants you to keep the knife."

We carried on talking a while, the old man eagerly showing us more items that he'd taken from the Russians. Most of them were just harmless souvenirs—a hat, some basic kit that any soldier would have—but there were several unexploded grenades and ordnance that really concerned me. I tried to get Vitaly to tell the man to take care and make sure that none of the kids ever went close to those. Vitaly gave me a look that said he'd had the same conversation with the old man many, many times.

We said goodbye and drove back through the quiet streets. Everywhere I looked I could see scars of the Russians' occupation, but for every burned or bombed-out house there were signs of Ukrainian resiliency. Blue-and-yellow flags hung everywhere, rubble had been cleared, and one guy was carefully mowing the lawn that surrounded his decimated house, while plumes of smoke rose into the sky behind him. These people may have been beaten, but they were far from broken.

We were almost out of Bucha when Vitaly mentioned that he wanted to take me to a certain street. The atmosphere in the car tensed, and as soon as we pulled up, I understood why.

The road was maybe a thousand feet long. At the far end was a bridge, or what was left of one. Both the road and the bridge had been blown to rubble, and between us and the wreckage of the bridge were cars. I counted at least a hundred, all of them regular civilian sedans and hatchbacks. Not one single vehicle was military. Yet all of them had been destroyed.

For once, Vitaly didn't speak. It was up to Dimas to tell us what happened, though I could guess all too easily.

"They waited until people were leaving and the traffic was busy. First they blew out the bridge up ahead, creating a roadblock. Then they took out these vehicles at the back, preventing anyone from escaping. After that, they started shooting. Go. See for yourself."

I walked ahead. The bodies had been cleared, but the vehicles had been left there like headstones in a graveyard. Each vehicle had hundreds, if not thousands of bullet holes. The metal had been ripped apart and mangled; there was no possibility anyone would have survived.

I imagined the lives that had ended inside each vehicle. I pictured how helpless these civilians, many of them women and children, would have felt against the might of the Russian military.

Moms. Kids. Grandparents.

"Someone counted," said Dimas, walking beside me. "The Russians fired over one hundred thousand rounds here that day. They killed thousands of people. This is not war. This is genocide."

That one trip to Bucha made a deep impression on me, but it wasn't the only time I found myself feeling shocked by what the Russians were doing. One day I was asked by someone working in a similar capacity to Rysko to collect a certain backpack. I was told that it held six biohazard-secure containers, each filled with soil from a different town in Ukraine. I agreed, collected the backpack, and handed it over to the contact in Poland when the trip was over. Later I heard that all six of the samples tested positive for chemical weapons. Those six towns were all civilian areas with no military facilities. We had hand-carried smoking-gun evidence of war crimes, but like most of the atrocities that we were witnessing, it would never make mainstream news and reach the public.

Seeing the way Russian forces were deliberately targeting civilians made me even more convinced that we were on the right track. I was determined that we would continue to do everything possible to aid the rescue of civilians but also whatever we could to support the Ukrainian troops as they fought to defend their families, homes, and freedom from the Russian invasion.

While our new TOC was being set up in Kyiv, it was time to stage the boats. When we'd first hatched the plan for them, we'd always known that it wouldn't be enough to simply buy them, bring them over, and have them stored in a warehouse ready for the moment they were needed. We'd need to be meticulous in our planning, finding suitable staging points where they could be securely stored and brought out to be used to get people across safely and efficiently as part of a wider evacuation plan.

Dennis, Vitaly, and I loaded up the Zodiacs and their varying motors, then spent a few days traveling around the country checking locations that we'd provisionally chosen, carrying out feasibility studies and ultimately staging the boats. Vitaly introduced us to Stepan, who was Ukrainian military and had been given the task of finding ways to move civilians across rivers in the area. Assuming he knew nothing about boats, I launched into a basic but thorough explanation of the way the boats worked and why they were the ideal vessel for getting people across rivers.

"And one more thing," I said as I was finishing up. "They're constructed in a way that allows them to take a few bullets without sinking. Kinda cool, right?"

There was a brief silence while Stepan and Vitaly both looked at me like I was an idiot.

"Stepan here was in the Ukrainian equivalent of the Navy SEALs," said Vitaly. "I think he's got a pretty good idea of how boats work."

I apologized, Stepan told me to forget about it, and we got down to business. It didn't take long to demo the boats, and even less time for Stepan and Vitaly to see the value of the Torqeedo electric engines. The ability to move the rubber crafts loaded with ten to twelve people at approximately twenty knots in complete silence was a clear win. We worked together to identify a suitable location and stage a boat, along with gas and electric motors, solar panels, fuel bladders, and battery packs—but not before Dennis and I did a test drive of the boats and spent a little while on the water, like any pair of water-loving Recon Marines would do.

When the work was done, we returned to Kyiv and our new TOC. I was now fully determined that part of our mission in Ukraine needed to be the support of its soldiers through our Mighty Oaks program efforts. I was eager to talk it through and make plans.

"We want to go see some of the troops who are doing the fighting," I told Vitaly. "We want to bring them medical supplies and teach them how to use them and then talk to them about what they are experiencing."

Vitaly nodded. "Okay. We can do that."

"And food? Can we take MREs and snacks out with us?"

"Of course."

"But we want to serve them spiritually as well. We want to talk about resiliency, to let them know that God's with them in this, that they're on the right side of righteousness. We want to let them know that even though they are going to face some hard times, God will see them through."

Vitaly flashed his perfect-white smile. "I like that, brother. Let's do it!"

———— • ————

A couple of days later Vitaly and Costa Rica invited us along to an event in the center of downtown Kyiv.

"You'll meet some good people there," said Vitaly. "All the military chaplains will be there and you can talk to them after the event."

I didn't have much of a clue what to expect, so I was surprised when Dennis, Roman, and I showed up to an open-air church event in the city square with at least six hundred people present. Vitaly and Dimas were easy enough to spot in their Ukrainian military chaplain uniforms, and beyond them, tuning his guitar, was Costa Rica. For once he wasn't smiling. He looked dead serious. Like he was about to go into battle.

When it was time to begin, Vitaly stepped to the front and said a few words before Costa Rica led everyone in worship. I recognized some of the songs and was mesmerized by the sight of all those people, some with eyes closed, some on their knees. Many of them were in tears, most of them singing with every ounce of their passion and energy. There we were, gathered in the city that is famous as the home of the Russian Orthodox Church—in the shadow of buildings scarred by recent Russian attacks—and I had no doubt at all that I was among brothers and sisters in Christ.

When the singing was over, Vitaly invited some of the other chaplains to join him. Roman translated for me and Dennis, and we listened in awe and misty-eyed as a long stream of people took the opportunity to share their stories.

One chaplain spoke of how he had witnessed Ukrainian forces being outnumbered by Russians shooting from all directions, but not one bullet hit them. He declared that God was protecting them.

Someone else described being with troops who had suffered heavy losses early in the week but who served with resilience and took the fight to the invading Russians. By the end of the week the Ukrainians had pushed them back and retaken an occupied section of Kharkiv.

There were stories of healings and near-misses, of implausible rescues and outrageous acts of grace. Each chaplain who spoke echoed the same truth: all of Ukraine should be proud of their troops and continue to pray for them.

But there was pain in the midst of the joy.

"When we pushed the Russians out of the village, there was nobody left alive . . ."

"They're taking people to the forest and shooting them at the side of giant open graves they have dug."

"They went for the women first. When they were finished, none of them were untouched."

As the testimonies moved between joy and sorrow, the atmosphere grew thicker. I could feel the weight of all this pain and the desperate need for God to step in and save people.

When there was nobody left who wanted to speak, it was time to pray. Vitaly led initially, but soon it was a chorus of cries and calls out to God, every voice lifted up. I joined them, too, asking God to help, offering myself to be used however He wanted. But my voice sounded small compared to everyone else's. And I knew that I needed to listen, not speak.

Listen to the chaplains.

Listen to the people.

Listen to God.

I could see from Dennis's face that he felt the same.

Soon I got to thinking: Everything I'd seen since coming to Ukraine, especially since we moved the TOC, told me that now more than ever the Russians were deliberately targeting civilians. Bucha wasn't a mistake or indiscriminate fire; it was a tactic. All those attacks on sedans and homes and pizza restaurants and hospitals were not the collateral damage of war. They were carefully targeted strikes and part of a deliberate strategy. Yes, the Ukrainian military were in the firing line, but so were the defenseless civilians. The war had started with Putin talking about how he wanted to liberate Ukraine. Everything I had witnessed told me that his real intention was to destroy it, and that included its people.

All this started me thinking about David and Goliath. An oppressive regime, determined to overwhelm and annihilate a neighbor, uses fear as their main weapon. No other story in the Bible fit quite as well. And just like the Israelites, the Ukrainians had no option other than to show up on the field of battle and defend themselves. They were smaller, weaker, and didn't have the right equipment, and the enemy was way better resourced. The odds were against them, but they had no choice other than to fight.

I've seen war, but never like what I saw in Ukraine. I've seen civilians attacked, but never with the arsenal of a world superpower. I've never seen the full force of a developed nation unleashed on civilians of another developed nation who have no means to defend themselves.

Putin's actions backed the people of Ukraine into a corner. He was so aggressive and so intent on destruction that he forced the Ukrainian people to rise up and resist him. He made a mockery of his own claims to want to liberate them and gave them a reason to fight back and risk their lives in the process. Putin played the part of Goliath, an enemy they could unite against, and the people of Ukraine were doing just that.

There in the city square, surrounded by hundreds of worshippers, I realized that God wasn't just looking for one shepherd boy who was prepared to stand up and fight. He was gathering a whole army of Davids, everyday people who were going to place their trust in Him, no matter what the cost.

It was an honor to worship God shoulder to shoulder with them.

EIGHT

INTO THE RED ZONE

AUGUST 6, 2022
Kharkiv, Ukraine

Between April and August we were busy. We made a number of trips to rescue more people, distribute medical supplies, and provide more resiliency training for frontline troops. At one point I made a trip with Dennis, Korey, and Jeremy Stalnecker—a former Marine Infantry Commander and cofounder of Mighty Oaks—to Kyiv to liaise with Samaritan's Purse, local chaplains, and other NGOs in providing frontline medical care. It was an ambitious project, working together to turn our six-wheeler into a mobile field hospital to treat troops injured on the front line.

All that travel and all those trips added up, and by the time we started discussing a two-week trip in August, I was ready to let someone else take charge of planning and preparation for the upcoming operation. Hunter stepped up and spent weeks putting together a detailed plan for a fourteen-day trip to the red zone—the front line of the battle in eastern Ukraine. But one dumb decision from me was all it took to undo so much of his good work.

We'd been back in Houston when I messed things up, though at the time I had no idea what I'd done. Kathy was away and it was a couple of days before we were due to fly out. Seaspray was still in Kyiv, but the rest of the team for the upcoming trip were all in my house, eating steaks, ignoring vegetables, and listening as Hunter gave an excellent brief of the kit he had assembled for us.

As always, the quality of guys in the room was exceptional. There was Dennis, Reed Hasty (an army combat engineer), and two former Navy SEALs—Luis Rivera and Colin Fields. All four were Mighty Oaks instructors. Bo was also coming back to Ukraine for the first time since Ben and Pierre's evac and would be leading the team on the ground. And even though Hunter was briefing combat veterans with decades of experience and expertise gained from operating at the highest level of special operations, he wasn't fazed. He was clear, confident, and executed his role to perfection.

The group, plus a few others from the Mighty Oaks staff, had just completed a mandatory training package we had put together, partnering with Fieldcraft Survival and Summit Point training. We'd covered topics like TCCC (Tactical Combat Casualty Care), survival, navigation, communications, defensive and evasive driving, off-road driving and vehicle self-recovery, foreign weapons familiarization, and the operational environment of Ukraine. This also included practicing teaching classes, as they would be expected to teach those we had the opportunity to minister to. It was great training and the team was ready to go.

Hunter had created identical sets of gear for all of us, and he'd thought of everything. There was camping equipment, satellite phones, GPS devices, maps, emergency contacts, charts, and contingency plans. The guys didn't have to worry about anything. Hunter had also prepared all the plans for once we got on the ground, coordinating with Vitaly to identify troops that we could meet with. We'd be heading east, getting close to the fighting, so everything was fluid and subject to change at the last minute, but Hunter had it all under control. Together with Dennis he gave a phenomenal operation brief followed by Bo, who gave a leader's brief, and Colin (who was not only a SEAL but an 18 Delta Special Forces–trained medic and a paramedic), who ran a refresher on the use of all our medical gear. We were ready to go.

My mistake was to mess with the plan.

"I'm not so sure about flying into Frankfurt," I said. "I've gone through there enough times already, and there are always delays and lost baggage. Let's do Heathrow instead."

Hunter gave me an *Okay, you're the boss* look and said he'd make the change for all of them, but it would be tough to change things for me because I had other meetings en route.

"That's fine," I said. "We can meet in Krakow."

Three days later we were all there. I rolled into the hotel with my bags after flying through Frankfurt without a delay. For Hunter and the team, on the other hand, things were not so smooth. They made it to Poland via London, but the airline didn't have a clue where their luggage was. We had a little more intel than they did, as the trackers that Hunter and Dennis had placed in the bags told them they were stuck in Heathrow.

All the equipment for the operation was a thousand miles away from where we needed it, and there was no indication we would get it anytime soon. All we could do was roll with it. We could put together basic kits out of what we could buy in Krakow and what we had at the TOC in Kyiv. It wasn't going to be perfect, but we would improvise and press forward.

Hunter was nothing but gracious and dealt with the problem without complaint. For the hundredth time I was impressed by the man my son had become. I felt bad for overstepping and telling him to change their route. Hindsight is a kick in the butt sometimes.

———————

The next day we had a driver take us to the border where we took a train to Lviv, where we had vehicles staged to drive to Kyiv. Seaspray met us at the TOC, though he wasn't going to join us on the trip. Vitaly showed up, and together we shared everything we knew about the latest Russian movements and Ukrainian response and set about planning the days ahead.

On our previous trip the Russians had already been changing the focus of their attack. Having failed to take Kyiv, they had stepped up their attacks in the east, starting with a missile strike that had hit a train station in Kramatorsk in early April. It had wounded more than one hundred civilians and killed at least fifty, including women and children. The attack had been followed by further assaults in the area, and by the time we were meeting in Kyiv—staring at our maps and plotting the latest intel—our eyes were drawn to an area at the edge of the eastern quarter of the country. The worst of the war was now being fought in an area that ran from Kharkiv in the north down through the towns of Izyum, Bakhmut, and Donetsk all the way south to Dnipro, Zaporizhzhia, and the coastal city of Mariupol.

Many of these places were already familiar to us. It had been widely reported that Ukraine's second-largest city, Kharkiv, had been under attack since the start of the war. Russia had rained down Grad missiles, Kalibr cruise missiles, and cluster bombs from afar, taking out apartment blocks and many other nonmilitary targets. The assault had failed, but the fighting on the outskirts continued throughout the summer. I'd heard reports that by now the death toll in the region was in the tens of thousands.

Mariupol was on the verge of being seized by the Russians. In just two months they had killed twice the number of residents that the Nazis had slaughtered when they occupied the city for two years during World War II.

Then there was Zaporizhzhia, home to the biggest nuclear power plant in Europe. It provided power to millions of households across Ukraine and was a prime target, with the Kremlin wanting to reroute the power it produced down to Crimea. The plant had fallen to Russian troops at the end of March, but there were rumors that the Ukrainian counteroffensive was imminent.

"First we go to Kharkiv," said Vitaly when our planning session was almost over. "Then we head south. Dnipro first, then Zaporizhzhia."

I looked around. Nobody flinched. This was the red zone, the place where the Ukrainian troops were exposed to the fiercest fighting and the civilians subjected to the most brutal abuses. This was where we needed to go.

Vitaly brought along Costa Rica and Dimas, as well as a nineteen-year-old kid called Alan. He was training to become a chaplain, and out of all the Ukrainians he spoke the best English, so he became the designated translator.

Traveling with Vitaly meant that checkpoints were no longer anywhere near as challenging as they had been early on. With his national connections, most times Vitaly was able to phone ahead and notify whoever happened to be in charge in the region that we were coming. Even when he couldn't do that, he, Costa Rica, and Dimas were able to talk with whoever was nervously guarding the road and put them at ease, especially since they were wearing their Ukrainian military chaplain uniforms.

Our drive from Kyiv over to Kharkiv was the calmest, easiest journey yet—which was kind of ironic given that our destination was almost totally surrounded by Russian forces. If Kharkiv was in the center of a clock face, the Russian forces were solid from nine all the way around to six. That left a small gap, which was still controlled by the Ukrainians, allowing us to get in and—hopefully—out again.

We'd timed the drive so that we'd arrive in the middle of the night, minimizing our chances of becoming a Russian target. It was around midnight when we rolled through deserted city streets. All the electricity was shut off, as it had been every night since the start of the war, and there was no cloud cover. It was strange to be surrounded by freeways and car dealerships and yet be able to look up and see a canopy of stars as bright and detailed as any I'd seen in rural mountains.

Driving slowly with our lights off, hesitant and braced for whatever might be around the next corner, we were all silent. Much of the city had been turned to rubble, and the residents had either fled, been killed, or were in hiding. The whole place was deserted, and it felt eerily like some zombie movie.

"There's nobody here," said Dimas over the radio, trying to break the tension. "Just maybe Will Smith and his dog" (a reference to the apocalypse movie *I Am Legend*).

We pressed on, navigating our way through to the eastern side of the city in the dark. Around 1:00 a.m. we finally reached our destination and stopped outside a large, still-intact concrete building, where we were rushed indoors by two nervous-looking men we could barely see—any lights could make us a target. We followed them deep into the center of the building—a windowless auditorium with hundreds of people sleeping in it.

I had the same uncomfortable feeling that I'd had in Pastor Bohdan's basement, and told Vitaly that I'd be happier sleeping upstairs.

He frowned. "They say the Russians usually start shelling at 4:00 a.m. Lately they've been getting close. You're sure?"

I told him I was and went off to find an empty room. I wasn't alone; the team all agreed with me.

Being able to sleep anywhere has plenty of advantages, but it also has some drawbacks. Like the fact that when the shelling started at 4:00 a.m., just like they'd said it would, I was fast asleep. I must have slept through the sirens, but I woke up to the sound of two blasts as the shells hit a nearby apartment block. I opened my eyes to see Dennis, up and alert.

"Come on!" he was yelling. "Chad! Reed! Luis! Colin! Body armor! Quick, put it on!"

Another explosion followed, this one maybe just five hundred yards away—close enough to make our building shake and rumble.

Dennis was still talking about body armor when a third impact landed, rattling the windows.

Our door opened. The two guys who had helped us into the building were there.

"No problem," one of them said, trying to reassure us. "Safe. Safe."

If we hadn't seen hundreds of flattened buildings on our way into Kharkiv I might have believed him. The impacts continued, steady and close every five to ten minutes in volleys of two to four. We listened out for a while, but eventually all of us lay back and tried to get some sleep. Even Dennis.

I must have dozed off for an hour or so when an even bigger blast woke me up. I grabbed my knife and a radio and headed downstairs looking for a bathroom. I saw Reed in one of the corridors, too, on the same mission as me. While navigating our way through the building with red-light headlamps, we stumbled on a soldier sleeping on some chairs. We gave each other a real scare, and the soldier jumped up in a panic. I reacted instinctively, pulling my knife out from the sheath. I was just about to stick it in the poor guy when I realized what was going on. I put my hands up, backed off, and left the soldier taking a bunch of deep breaths.

———————

Things were calmer in the morning. The shelling had paused, the sun was up, and we could finally explore the building we were staying in. As we wandered around, I saw it was some kind of theatre, with a large auditorium in the middle.

We found Vitaly and were introduced to some of the pastors. They insisted we share their breakfast, and as we ate Vitaly explained the significance of the place we were in.

"This building was a theatre," he'd said, "but it was not known for the plays or ballets that were performed here. In the old Soviet days this was the place where they would bring Christians. They would put them on trial and pass sentence. This was a place of Christian persecution, where some were sent to their death, but now it is a place of refuge for those who follow Jesus. God has a sense of humor, no?"

Soon after we'd finished breakfast, it was time to join the hundreds of people who had been sleeping in the building with us and file into the main auditorium for church. A woman was leading a small band playing worship songs, and the whole thing looked and sounded just like any regular Sunday service. I recognized some of the songs, and just like the open-air service in the heart of Kyiv, I was blown away by it all. These people had lost everything—husbands, kids, homes, security, jobs, freedom, everything—and yet here they were, worshipping God.

Would I do the same if my life got ripped apart? Could I be certain that I would be able to lift myself out of my own despair, fear, or remorse, and put my eyes on Jesus? Could I pause the panic and learn to trust God? I wasn't so sure that I could answer yes to any of those questions.

I was even more stirred up because, just as the service had been about to begin, Vitaly had asked whether I'd be willing to share a few words with everyone. There was no way I could have said no, but my heart was starting to pound. I've spoken in so many churches before, but what could I say to these people? I hadn't lost anything but they had lost everything. I had chosen to be there but they were trapped with nowhere to go. I couldn't even begin to relate to them, much less find the right words to encourage them.

With each new song I could feel myself swept up in the power of the moment. I wanted to say something profound, something that would match the mood and leave people encouraged. Maybe even inspired. But what?

"Hi," I said, when the singing ended and Vitaly invited me to the front. "Uh, well, I don't know what to say. I mean, I can't relate to what you're going through here. Our nation was attacked on September 11, 2001, but it wasn't the same. We fought in Afghanistan and our homes and our families were safe while we were away fighting. We didn't experience fighting in our own towns and from our homes and churches. I don't even know the loss that you all must feel. So, I guess what I want to say first is that I cannot relate to what you're going through, so I'm not going to pretend I do."

I hadn't planned any of this. But I was in too deep now to change.

"My friends that are here with me are the same. None of us really knows what you're going through. But all of us are here because of the same, simple reason: we're here because we care and we're here to help. And if nothing else we are here to let you know that you are not alone. People from around the world do care about you. And God . . . God loves you and there is no better place on the planet to be closer to Him right now than right where we are standing worshipping Him in the midst of this war."

It wasn't my best sermon. Maybe if I'd been preaching at a church back home I would have carried on. I might have started talking about the importance of not allowing partisan politics to put the brakes on our Christian compassion. I might have talked about having the courage not to let ourselves be swayed by mainstream media or political elites. Or how important it is that we learn to develop the kind of faith that pushes us out of our comfort zones, not the kind that barricades us against it.

But these people didn't need to hear any of that. They knew all about compassion and courage and being pushed out away from all the comforts they had previously relied on. They were the ones with the lessons to teach. They had the answers. All I could do was ask them how I could help.

As I sat down, I was thinking a lot about how events in Afghanistan and Ukraine had taught me that not knowing what to say should not be a barrier to action. Not knowing what to say shouldn't keep us away. Sometimes it's enough to be honest, to own the fact that we don't know what someone else is experiencing, and to offer our help. Sometimes just our presence is all that is needed. People can smell fake a mile off. But they can spot genuine love and heart just as easily.

We're so used to our consumer-driven way of living that it can feel weird to serve people this way. We can become so accustomed to treating God like a vending machine—punching in our prayer requests and waiting for Him to deliver the goods—that the idea of helping others with no fixed agenda or expectations on our end just feels plain wrong.

But it isn't wrong. We were made to be like this, to serve the way Jesus served: on His knees, washing feet, meeting people who are bruised and broken and who the rest of society wanted nothing to do with. We're called to do the same—to help the needy, the broken, the fearful, the sick, those who can't help themselves. We're called to give them what they need as an expression of the deep compassion and love that stir God's own heart.

So often we try to bring God into our vision and plan for our life, worshipping Him with the assumption that if we turn up to church often enough or sing with the right level of passion, He'll rubber-stamp our plan for our life. Instead, we need to take time to figure out His plan and join in on that.

When the service was over, we went with Vitaly, Costa Rica, and Dimas, as well as a man from church, and drove around Kharkiv. The roads were cratered and littered with rubble, and at times we could drive only at a walking pace.

It gave us plenty of time to study the damage.

Back before the war began, Kharkiv had been home to 1.5 million people. It was a major city, built for modern living. Yet the Russian missiles had dragged it back decades. High-rise apartment blocks had been decimated. Shopping malls turned into twisted piles of metal. Ice cream parlors reduced to broken signs and piles of rocks. Kids' playground equipment charred and melted. Dead bodies were trapped beneath crushed homes and apartment complexes. Even if not one more bomb fell, it would take years to put Kharkiv back together again.

But the destruction wasn't the only thing that struck me as we drove. It was the silence. We were there midmorning on a Wednesday, a time when the streets should have been full of the chaos of traffic and pedestrians and life being busy as usual. Instead, it was quiet. Eerily quiet. Like the Russians had just left or were hiding out of sight.

From time to time Vitaly would have us pull over and get out to see things up close. "Take photos," he'd say. "Show people what's happened here."

We did as he said, walking slowly and quietly, staring at the carnage all around us.

Eventually, someone asked the question that we had all been thinking. "Where is everyone?"

Vitaly stopped and turned around, like he was convinced he'd see people if he only looked hard enough. "Almost everyone has gone. Those who have stayed and live among the ruins know how to hide."

At one point we stopped to look at an unexploded rocket that was wedged, nose-down, in the sidewalk. It was strange to see it like that, and it looked kind of comical, so a bunch of us took turns having our photo taken standing next to it. After all that death and heaviness, we needed to smile and laugh a little. *(Just for the record, I highly discourage anyone from standing near UXO—Unexploded Ordnance—even if it does get you a great photo.)*

"Guys?" It was Luis. He was standing by the vehicle he'd been driving. It was the only armored truck we had in our convoy, and there was a problem.

"Does anyone have a spare key for this? I locked mine inside."

The laughter was brief when it became clear that he wasn't joking. A few guys kicked into fix-it mode while the rest of us stood around and waited.

Ironically Luis's truck was the only armored vehicle in the group. The thing about armored trucks is that they're not just designed to withstand bombs and bullets. They're made to resist all kinds of attacks, including getting in without a key. So after a few minutes of trying—and failing—to pick the locks, force down a window, and break in through the rear, the guys had to get creative. It took thirty or forty minutes, a bunch of improvised wedges—including a compression cuff—and a long wire to hook on to the lock latch before we could get inside and back on the road again.

Back at the theatre that evening, I spent a little more time in the basement. I wanted to sit with some of the people from the church, to breathe the same air as them. Maybe have a little of their faith rub off on me. But I got more than that.

I found myself talking with the woman who had been leading the worship earlier that day. She told me her name was Anna, and she was around my age. She looked and sounded like a regular soccer mom, and I told her that I'd enjoyed the service. When she responded, her words were nothing like the typical conversation I'd have over coffee after church at home.

"There is evil in the world," she began. "There is danger and violence and people who want to hurt and destroy you. And just because you put your trust in God for your children, your loved ones, and everyone else that you care about, doesn't mean that they are going to be safe. You understand?"

"I do." I started to share some of my experiences but stopped myself. This was a moment to listen and not speak.

"People say they trust God, but what they actually say is *I trust that God will*... They have a contract all drawn up, and they expect God to come through for them, exactly the way they want Him to. But really trusting God means letting go of the outcome. It means giving up on getting the results you want. And when you do that, everything changes. That's what you saw today.

"Almost everyone here is learning what it means to truly put our faith in God. And when the Russians came, we all started from the same place, telling God that we trusted Him to do what we wanted, to protect our children and loved ones. But everyone here has lost someone they loved. Some of the people you were worshipping alongside have seen their own children shot to death, blown up, or executed. But they're still here. They're still believing that God exists and is with us. And they're finding that God can take their rage and their sorrow and their pain. He can take it all. Every tear and every shout. He is enough."

This was a lesson I desperately needed to learn. It was also one that I would soon be tested on.

NINE

"WHAT ARE YOU HERE FOR?"

We headed south into no-man's-land—the strip that ran from Kharkiv in the north down to Mariupol in the south. On any given day nobody was completely sure who controlled what town or territory in eastern Ukraine. All we could do was gather our intel, plan good routes, keep alert, and trust that whatever happened, God would be right there with us.

Vitaly had arranged for us to spend a few hours with a unit of combat engineers just north of Dnipro. It took several hours to drive the hundred miles from Kharkiv, and another little while to find the patch of forest where the engineers were based. I spent much of the drive thinking about the troops we were going to see. We were loaded up with supplies for them—medical gear including IFAKs (Individual First Aid Kits), water purification filters, and various snacks. I was confident that they'd appreciate the supplies but wondered how they'd respond to us in general. Soldiers, by nature, form tight-knit groups, and they don't always respond well to strangers coming in—especially when the troops are focused on combat operations.

A bigger unknown for me involved the fact that this trip was under the banner of Mighty Oaks, unlike previous rescue operations. We were there to support troops and talk about the four pillars of resiliency, especially the spiritual pillar. As a Christian nonprofit we talk a lot about having a relationship with Jesus and how it can bring peace in times when it seems peace is nowhere to be found. We share our testimonies and talk about war, hardship, and God's love and mercy. We're unapologetically Christian, and I wasn't sure how we'd be received.

After a couple of hours driving through the forest, passing through several checkpoints, we finally arrived. The camp was in the middle of the woods, directly on the front line, with fighting positions dug in all around. The unit leadership seemed excited to have us there, and as Alan stepped in, translating and making the introductions, I was starting to feel confident that the visit would go well.

The men were poorly equipped, with mismatched uniforms, twenty-year-old ballistic vests, aging weapons, and subpar equipment. Additionally, they looked tired, both mentally and physically. But as soon as we started handing out the IFAKs and supplies, they lost any hint of suspicion. They eagerly lined up and looked excited that someone cared enough to visit them and bring needed supplies.

We didn't have long, so we quickly started on the Mighty Oaks talks. As these men were engineers, we'd given Reed—a former army combat engineer and Iraq veteran—the task of delivering the first presentation. Before he'd got more than a minute in, I was feeling emotional.

I'd first met Reed ten years earlier. I was in Broken Arrow, Oklahoma, for the weekend, giving a Brazilian jiu-jitsu seminar on Saturday and speaking at a local church on Sunday. These were the early days of Mighty Oaks, and I still hadn't gotten over the shock of how poorly the country was caring for its veterans. Everywhere I went I was meeting vets who had been diagnosed with PTSD, given no meaningful support, and felt as though their lives were spiraling down. Broken Arrow was no different.

Reed was at the jiu-jitsu seminar, and again at church the next day. I saw him from the pulpit as I spoke, and I could tell he was engaged. We met after the service and he told me that he was a combat veteran who had been diagnosed with PTSD and had been experiencing panic attacks. He'd been in and out of the VA inpatient clinics and spent weekends in the local psych ward, where they'd dose him up on meds and put him on suicide watch.

"They used to trust me with equipment worth millions of dollars," he said. "Now they won't even trust me with my shoelaces."

He told me that he loved what I was saying about Mighty Oaks, and that he'd like to come to one of our programs—not just for himself but to be part of the solution for others. I told him that we'd love to have him, and we traded contact info to make it happen.

Reed's panic attacks were so severe and unpredictable that it took him six months before he was able to board a plane in Tulsa and make it out to one of our programs in California. But when he finally showed up, he was ready. He completed the program, surrendered his life to Christ, and saw things begin to change. Soon he signed up for our leadership training and went on to become first a Mighty Oaks instructor, then eventually our lead instructor trainer. Over the years he has led thousands of men like him to Christ, discipling them to do the same.

Sitting in the forest on the front lines of the Ukraine war and watching Reed share his testimony was something I will never forget. He was speaking to over a hundred combat engineers, and he was confident and clear. His message was full of hope, and it exemplified everything that I had envisioned when I'd started Mighty Oaks back in 2011. It was never simply about helping veterans; it was about giving them purpose again, showing them where to find true healing, then letting them get to a position to turn around and show the next guy—paying it forward. It's the last thing Jesus commanded us to do when He said, "Go forth and make disciples of others."

Watching Reed, I got choked up. I consider it one of the greatest privileges in life that God would allow me to see someone make such an incredible recovery.

Reed's talk impacted not only me but the Ukrainians too. They sat and listened to his story in perfect silence, then when he was done they drowned him in questions and praise. These men were very much like us, and in that moment any insecurities as to whether we brought value to them or not was gone.

A friend of mine, Ivan, runs a partner organization called Sports Catalyst, and he'd given us a box of audio Bible sticks with earbuds. When the last question had been asked and answered, we mentioned the Bible sticks. The guys crowded forward to get theirs, and I'm sure everyone took one.

I spoke with a couple of other groups while Hunter and the guys taught them how to use the IFAKs and water filter systems. We ended with a meal—stew cooked over an outdoor fire—then said our good-byes, prayed, and were on our way.

We drove south from Dnipro. Vitaly had arranged for us to stay in an inn for the night so that we could approach Zaporizhzhia early the next day. Unlike Kharkiv, where it was safest to arrive under the cover of darkness, Vitaly was clear that we needed to arrive at our next host in daylight. They needed to see who was coming. Otherwise, things could get interesting—in other words, according to Vitaly, "We probably will get shot."

"They are called Safari," he explained to me when we stopped the next morning to buy a load of pizzas in the nearest town. "And they are not like other units. They are . . . special. The unit was created by a guy called Baton. He's like the Dana White of Ukrainian MMA and former Ukrainian Special Forces from the 2014 war. When the invasion happened, Baton was asked to create a special unit that would cause chaos among the Russians—basically a hit squad. He used his influence and contacts to reach out to all the coaches for the MMA fighters, boxers, wrestlers, and martial arts grapplers. He brought them and their athletes together and the level of comradery they have is hard to find. But . . ."

Vitaly paused, like he wasn't sure whether what he was about to say was okay.

"Safari is tough, but they need military training. That's why Baton and the men of Safari are so excited to meet you. You are a professional fighter from StrikeForce and Bellator, and you were special operations who fought in Afghanistan. If they like you and the team, maybe we can come back again and help them more."

Our visit with the combat engineers had gone so well. After everything I'd just heard about Safari, I wasn't so sure that we could expect the same kind of response. Elite athletes and military members are typically alphas with big egos and often closed-minded. I suspected these Safari guys would be difficult to break through to, but I was game to try.

———

The moment we arrived at what looked like an abandoned factory in the middle of the countryside, it was obvious that Vitaly had not been exaggerating. The men of Safari were nothing like the engineers we'd just visited with in Dnipro. The soldier who let us in the gate was jacked and looked like a top-ten welterweight on the UFC roster. In fact, everyone seemed like they were in peak physical condition, and there were more cauliflower ears among them than any D1 college wrestling room. And while they weren't a formally trained special operations unit, they'd been given top-grade weapons and equipment.

I immediately had the feeling that these were my people. There's something about being among combat-sports athletes, a mutual respect and brotherhood that goes beyond nationality. I hoped they felt the same about us and that our commonalities would help to earn their trust. But the moment Vitaly introduced us to Baton—whose name means "concrete"—it was clear it wasn't going to be as easy as showing the men a few BJJ moves, sharing a war story or two from my days in Afghanistan, and getting an open-arms welcome to the tribe.

Baton looked unimpressed. He was about six feet three, built like a tank, and stared down at me with a gaze that made it clear he didn't have any interest in what we had to say. He whispered something to one of his guys, then walked off.

"Come," said Vitaly, who for the first time ever was subdued and appeared almost nervous. "Baton wants this guy to show you around."

We did what we were told and followed the guy into the building. At some point in the past it must have been a metal fabrication plant, but now it looked specially designed for the four hundred fighters and coaches that made up Safari. There were guys wearing body armor doing pull-ups on the rusted beams that crossed the ceiling while others (also wearing their armor) were running laps up and down the wide metal staircase at the side. If Hollywood wanted a location for the scene of an MMA war film, this was perfect.

Our tour took us down to the basement where the members of Safari lived. Upstairs was cool, but what lay beneath it was even more impressive.

"This whole place was an old Soviet steel factory," said Vitaly as we passed through metal doors that were at least twelve inches thick. "Down here was a secret bomb shelter, designed to withstand a nuclear blast from the Americans."

We looked in on the storeroom. Gas masks that were decades old were piled up on the shelves, next to Safari's own stocks of high-end body armor, helmets, uniforms, night-vision scopes, and quality weapons and ammunition. The walls were covered in classic Soviet-era anti-American propaganda, with maps of the US showing primary targets: New York; Washington, DC; Denver, Colorado; and other strategic American sites.

When the tour was over, we went back upstairs and were shown to a long table outside where Baton was waiting for us. As we were about to sit down, we heard the sound of indirect fire landing nearby, maybe a few thousand yards away. Everyone stopped for a moment, assessing the distance and frequency. After a minute or two one of Baton's senior guys waved the all clear, and we all took our seats.

Vitaly was clearly on edge, and he asked some of his guys to bring out the pizzas we'd brought with us. We sat in silence as they were collected from the vehicle and laid on the table.

Nobody moved until Baton grabbed a slice. And even then, there was silence.

"We're in the middle of a war," Baton said to me when he had finished his mouthful. "We don't have time for preachers and we don't really need pizzas. What are you here for?"

I was put on the spot, but I welcomed it. I held his gaze and answered Baton as honestly as I could.

"I don't really know why we are here," I started. "Other than I believe God burdened our hearts to do something to come and help. We had our 9-11, but our country has never been invaded. All of my team here have seen combat, we've all lost friends and seen war, but we can't relate to what you are experiencing as you fight for your homes and protect your families. We won't claim to understand what you are dealing with, but I can say that we are sitting here on the front line with you at this table not because we understand but because we care. We are here to let you know that you're not alone."

Baton sat in silence a while, then said simply, "I understand."

Then out of left field he asked, "Who is monitoring the GPSs you guys are carrying?"

"They're on our own network."

He paused again. Everyone waited.

"You were in the Afghanistan war. I want to know your story. Tell me."

"Okay," I said, but before I could begin Baton pointed at Alan and ordered him to translate so that all his men could hear.

I talked about how I felt after 9-11, about my experiences in Afghanistan, about losing friends and the lessons I've taken from twenty years of combat. I was transparent, pulling back the curtain of my life. I talked about how hard it was to come home and be normal again. I talked about dealing with anxiety, depression, anger, and panic attacks. I talked about my struggles as a husband and a father, how I came so close to suicide but finally made it through after giving my life to Jesus and starting to live life the way God intended. I spoke about the thousands of warriors who came to Mighty Oaks over the past decade, and how I learned from them that we all struggle with similar battles no matter how different we may think we are.

And then I went back to my initial words: "And God burdened our hearts to be with you. We want to help. We want you to know that you are not alone. We are right here, and God is with us all as this evil invades your land and threatens your families and freedom. We want you to know that politics and governments aside, you're in a just war—a war of good against evil. You're on the right side of it, but you're going to face losses. You're going to lose friends, but you're not going to have the time to grieve those losses. To be effective in defending your country you're going to have to push on through it all, but some of those losses are really going to impact the souls of your men. We're here to help you with that. We know how to help prepare your men to be resilient, so that when this is all over one day and you go home, the experience here won't destroy you."

Baton listened carefully, frowning. Then, "Yeah."

It didn't sound like an agreement. More like an answer to a

conversation he was having in his own head. Then he took a bite of his pizza and looked around at his men one by one. Only when he was finished chewing did he continue.

"Some of our guys are already struggling."

There was another pause, even longer this time.

"We have good weapons and equipment here already. And our guys are tough fighters too, so we don't need help with that. But they're not soldiers. They could use some advice on tactics to stay safe when we fight, and they need medical supplies and training. These are things we need from you. These, and the lessons you just shared."

"Yeah," I said. "Of course. We can help with that."

Baton stared at me. I made sure I maintained eye contact.

"Thank you," he said.

And that was it. Baton looked each of us over, smiled just a fraction, and nodded. We were in.

"But," he said, standing up and nodding to one of his guys, "maybe first we should do one thing. Vitaly says one of your men is a sniper, yes?"

I looked at Dennis, who nodded back. "Yeah," I said. "Dennis is our guy."

"We have one too." Baton pointed to a tall, slender soldier, who replied with a stoic nod. "Klym. He's killed many Russians. We shall see who is better."

The conversation I'd had with Baton was the first hurdle, but this was the second. Ten minutes later we were back inside a different part of the factory, standing at one end of an improvised shooting range and watching as someone placed two cans at the other end of a long, low building. It must have been four hundred yards end to end—not a difficult shot for a seasoned Force Recon Scout Sniper like Dennis, but the pressure was on, especially as Dennis would be shooting someone else's rifle.

A couple dozen Safari guys were gathered around Klym, slapping the back of the rangy-looking soldier. If there was ever a stereotypical-looking sniper, Klym was him. He offered Dennis his rifle and asked him to shoot first.

Dennis wasn't falling for it. "No, no, no," he said. "No way! It's your rifle and it's zeroed to you. You shoot first."

Klym shrugged and gave Dennis a smirk, loaded the rifle, and climbed onto the bed of a camouflaged pickup truck that someone had driven into the warehouse. He took his time as he placed the rifle's bipod on the roof of the cab, methodically chambered a round, slowed his breathing, and melted into position to squeeze off his shot.

Boom!

Dennis spotted for him. "Hit."

Baton was standing with his arms crossed. As all the Safari men cheered for their guy, Baton just smiled.

Dennis congratulated Klym, took the rifle, and climbed up into the back of the truck, mimicking the position of the Ukrainian before him. He took his time, checking the rifle over, settling into the scope, and relaxing into position. Dennis is a highly respected Marine Scout Sniper instructor, who had even been hand-selected to teach at the US Army Special Forces Sniper course. He served in Iraq for both the Marine Corps and as a government contractor. I had no doubt in his ability to take out targets on the battlefield, but here, with the pressure of Baton, Safari, and all of our team watching? There was a real chance that Dennis might have been under more pressure right now than if he was in real combat.

Dennis took his time. He slowed his breathing. He melted into his final firing position. Only when he was ready did he squeeze off his own shot.

Boom!

Klym raised his head from the spotting scope, looked at Dennis, and smiled without saying a word. Then the sniper looked back at Baton. His English accent was thick but clear.

"Hit."

Baton smiled, uncrossed his arms, and started clapping. Soon all of the Safari men joined in loud celebration, hugs, and laughter. We could all live with a draw. More important, we had made a bond, and from that moment on we were welcome as part of Safari.

———————

For the next two days our guys were spread among Baton's unit. All of us spent hours hanging out, talking, sharing gear, giving advice, training, and demonstrating things that we'd picked up through years of training and combat. Hunter spent a long time demonstrating how to use the water filters we'd brought, and of course Hunter and I got to do a little wrestling with some of the men, trading techniques and sharing old stories.

Even though they were well equipped, Safari still had the same problems with medical kits and training that every other unit in the Ukrainian military had. They were particularly interested in the type of IFAKs we carried since theirs were big and bulky, with outdated supplies. Ours had way better contents and were specially designed to slimly fit beneath our body armor inside the plate carriers.

All throughout our time there I could hear our Mighty Oaks guys—Dennis, Reed, Luis, Colin, and Hunter—sharing parts of their own stories and talking about the importance of being spiritually strong, just like I'd heard all of them do countless times in our programs back home with American veterans and servicemembers. It was organic and authentic, not forced in any way. We'd given some of the Bible sticks out to the engineers but still had a lot left. The more our guys shared their stories with Safari, the more we saw them go over to the box and help themselves to the audio Bibles.

When our time was up, I assured Baton that we'd return in September with more IFAKs for his men, and that we'd give them the full medical training they needed to use them properly.

"We're gonna come back and take care of you guys," I said. "In the meantime you and all the guys will be in our prayers, but can we pray with you all before we go?"

"Please," Baton said and we stood together—American and Ukrainian friends with our hands over each other's shoulders—and prayed in both languages for God's hand of protection.

"Thank you," he said, giving me a firm handshake and patting my shoulder.

Vitaly was buzzing as we loaded up and got ready to drive off. "How many of those Bible sticks do you have left?"

I checked. "None. The boxes are empty."

"Really? How many were in there?"

"Over a thousand."

"Amazing," he said.

"How come?"

"The last time I was with anyone who tried to hand out anything Christian like that, nobody took a single thing. Safari really likes you guys."

———

Our next stop was in the city of Mykolaiv, down where the Dnipro River meets the Black Sea. Vitaly had made contact with the chaplain of a unit whose mission was responding to a Russian warship that was launching missile attacks around the region. We'd planned on meeting the chaplain first, then spending a day with the troops. But theirs was a fluid situation, and midway into the drive, when we'd stopped to refuel, Bo and I got a call from Seaspray.

The Ukrainians had just rocketed a Russian airfield, and there was solid intel that the retaliatory attacks would include the nuclear plant just south of where we were headed. To make matters worse, the winds were consistently blowing north. You never want to be near a nuclear plant being bombed, and you especially don't want to be upwind of one.

It wasn't good news. Russia had already shown they were willing to launch missiles at nuclear facilities when they'd taken the Chernobyl plant in the north early on in the war. They'd been unbelievably reckless in their attack, sending the world into panic, and they'd been lucky not to cause a full-scale nuclear disaster. If they were running that same play again, we needed to be cautious.

Vitaly got on a call with the chaplain and confirmed Seaspray's intel. We checked the map and our weather apps. The nuclear facility was less than eighty miles away. If there had been a leak, there was a strong wind blowing whatever radiation might be spewing out of it right toward us.

I glanced at Bo. His face mirrored exactly how I felt.

"We're not going, are we?" I said.

"No. It doesn't look good."

I told the rest of our guys, who took the news like I'd expect them to receive any FRAGO (fragmentary order) of a change in operations: they were calm, accepting, and waited until it was clear what we would be doing next.

Vitaly's response was different.

"Really?" he said, his face twisting into a bemused smile and looking around sarcastically, like he was trying to see the potential radioactive particles in the air. "It doesn't seem too bad to me. Are you sure?"

"Yes. I am. So I need you to help me find a link-up point with the chaplain so we can at least drop off the supplies for the soldiers."

Vitaly looked at me, clearly reluctant to change plans. I got it. I understood. But I was not willing to expose the team to that level of risk.

"Okay," he said eventually. "It's the right call."

We drove toward the outskirts of Mykolaiv, where we'd arranged to meet the chaplain. We kept alert but didn't see any of the Russian forces rumored to be patrolling in the area. Even so, when we arrived at the location, we did as the chaplain had advised and parked the vehicles at the rear of an abandoned apartment block. We walked the final block quietly, carrying our boxes of supplies and keeping careful lookout.

The chaplain was clearly relieved as he ushered us inside a residential courtyard and closed the heavy metal gate behind us. "You didn't see any Russians, did you?"

"None."

"That's good. They've been patrolling all day, sometimes getting as close as the next block."

Once we were inside the house, we showed him what we had brought for the unit: some food and a few water filters, as well as the last of our med supplies. I apologized for not having any Bible sticks, but the chaplain wasn't able to focus. The stress he was under was clear, and he was on edge and unable to relax the whole time we were there.

"Could we pray for you?" asked Luis.

For the first time, the chaplain appeared to relax. "Please," he sighed, dropping down to his knees, lifting his hands skyward. Each of us put a hand on his shoulders, and a few of us took turns praying for him and his soldiers. He was fighting back the tears.

"Thank you," he said as soon as we were done. "But now, please, you should go. It's not safe for you to stay here."

We walked back to the vehicles in the darkness, looking and listening for the Russian patrols. I could hear several heavy diesel engines in the distance, but none of them were close enough to worry me.

The worry only kicked in when we started driving.

Out of nowhere a series of explosions lit up the dark night sky ahead of us. We pulled over on the side of a long country highway surrounded by open fields and made some calls to see if we could gather any more intel on the attacks. Bo and I studied our maps by flashlight on the hood of one of the vehicles, trying to assess route options back to Kyiv. The explosions and flashes continued, and from the sound and direction, they were pretty heavy incoming ordnance, landing about one mile south of our position. Bo and I were deep in our route survey on the map when I heard laughing behind me.

I looked. It was Alan, Costa Rica, Dimas, and Vitaly. All four of them were standing in the middle of the road, dancing as Costa sang what sounded to me like a hip-hop folk tune.

I was confused, but only momentarily. People have all different ways of breaking tension. I'm not a dancer, but I guess if I were, I'd have joined in.

I went back to the map with Bo but then turned back again. "Hey, Luis. Didn't you do a little break dancing when you were younger?"

Luis didn't need a formal invitation. He handed me his body armor and demonstrated, right there on the asphalt, just how good of a break-dancer he had been. The back spins and helicopters set everyone cheering, and Dimas responded with a couple of backflips of his own.

The bombs continued falling, but the guys kept their dance-off going. For a moment the sound of explosions in the distance was drowned out by our cheers and laughter. For a moment, all was well in the world.

TEN

RISKING IT ALL

SEPTEMBER 25, 2022
Izyum and Bakhmut, Ukraine

I was back at home for much of September, putting together plans for another trip to Ukraine at the end of the month—my tenth visit since the start of the war. Most waking hours of every day I kept a careful eye on the news, especially when Ukraine launched a rapid counteroffensive in the northeastern Kharkiv region. It sent Russian units into retreat, and on September 10, Zelensky's troops finally raised the Ukrainian flag on the city of Izyum. This was a significant victory, Izyum having been occupied by Russian forces for six months. People were talking of the victory being a turning point in the war, and I could easily see why. I could also imagine how much terror and suffering the people of Izyum must have endured during those long months of Russian occupation.

The Ukrainian fightback wasn't just limited to Izyum, however. They successfully pushed Russian forces back all over the region, reclaiming thousands of square miles. Putin's response revealed his desperation. In addition to attacking the Ukrainian infrastructure, leaving many without power and water, he also announced a "partial mobilization" of three hundred thousand troops to fight in Ukraine, triggering a mass flight of Russians escaping conscription by fleeing into neighboring Georgia and Kazakhstan. Putin was also accused of forcibly deporting hundreds of thousands of Ukrainian citizens in what the US claimed was a "series of horrors."

With all this taking place, we kept our plans for the upcoming trip loose. We knew we were going to return to Zaporizhzhia to deliver the promised supplies and training to Safari, and there was another unit in

Bakhmut that Vitaly wanted us to spend time with, but beyond that plans were flexible.

Having already spent so much of 2022 away from home, I decided that this would be my last visit to Ukraine for the year. I needed to focus on Mighty Oaks as a whole, including our continued efforts to rescue people from Afghanistan. So the plan was for me to be on the trip, but tagging along rather than planning and pulling it together. That duty had now fallen to Hunter, who had more than proved himself already. All the same, turning the reins over to Hunter was a step that I couldn't have imagined taking six months earlier when I'd called him at home in the middle of the night and asked him to buy all that comms equipment. Back then I'd assumed that the only part he was going to play in Ukraine was the role of our FedEx guy.

Hunter had put together a great team, which included David (a MARSOC—Marine Special Operations Command—Raider), Steve (an ANGLICO Marine who Hunter had served with in Afghanistan), and "Doc Mac" (a trauma doctor from Ireland who worked with Fieldcraft Survival teaching emergency field medicine). The four of them complemented each other perfectly, and as far as I was concerned, Seaspray and I were just there to offer any support they needed.

Almost as soon as we arrived at the TOC in Kyiv and met up with Seaspray, the plan for me to hang back came under pressure. Seaspray received a call saying there was a US Marine who had been fighting for the Ukrainians. Reports suggested that he had been shot in the abdomen and was captured, but there was credible intelligence to suggest that there was the potential for him to be rescued if we were willing to go in and get him. Seaspray and I started to talk and assess the information we'd been given, figuring out quickly that if we were going to attempt an extraction, Izyum would be the most likely staging post.

Then, within the hour, we received another call.

I sat and watched Seaspray go through his routine, getting all the essential details as efficiently as possible. When he was done, he broke it down for me.

"There's a report of mass graves in Izyum. Fifteen hundred women and children. Rysko wants us to get eyes on to verify."

With billions of dollars flowing into Ukraine from the Biden White House, there was clearly an incentive for Ukraine to embellish or falsify reports of atrocities, so our government contacts wanted independent verification. If it was true, we needed to know. The world needed to know.

Both the rescue of the Marine and verification of the mass graves felt like exactly the kind of thing we were there to do, but saying yes to them would mean leaving Hunter to carry out his mission without me.

Do I leave Hunter to lead the operation without me by his side? Or do I give in to my desire to be a hovering dad and say no to Seaspray?

It was a question of trust, but not my trust of Hunter. It was about my own trust of God. Was I prepared to let go? Was I willing to put aside my own need to be there to protect my son and ensure his safety? Or was I okay with handing him over to God? Could I accept that the safest place Hunter could be was in the center of God's will, not under my own supervision?

After all I'd seen in Ukraine, I knew what I had to do. It was time to let go. Deep down—deeper than the fear I was sensing—I knew that I trusted Hunter, and I knew that I trusted God even more. As much as I love Hunter, God loves him more. As much as I want to protect Hunter, God can do it better.

So yes. It was time to risk it all. It was time to trust God.

Seaspray and I left the TOC that night, only a couple hours after receiving the first call about the captured Marine. It was just the two of us in the Land Cruiser, and we had the back loaded with enough supplies for us to live out of it for a week or two, along with all the necessary equipment for various rescue options to get the Marine. Additionally, we had one of Elon Musk's Starlink internet dishes on the roof and our trusty espresso machine ratcheted down in the floorboard in the back, both of which would come in handy along the way.

We weren't completely alone. Max—a Ukrainian cosmetic dentist who had become a chaplain after the invasion—had joined as our interpreter. He was following us in a box truck filled with supplies for the front line, courtesy of our friends at Samaritan's Purse.

I was excited for the operation and had a strong sense of peace about what lay ahead for us, as well as for Hunter's team. But we had a lot of miles between us and Izyum, and without Vitaly on board, our passage through checkpoints was going to be a challenge once again, especially the smaller checkpoints in rural locations manned by local militia. I did the math and worked out that it could take us up to ten hours to drive the four hundred miles from Kyiv to Izyum, and then a whole bunch of extra hours for checkpoints.

"More like eight hours total," said Seaspray, pointing to a laminated piece of paper that was taped to the dash. "Vadim sent me a pass."

As I've mentioned before, Vadim was the National Ukrainian Chief of Police and our main contact for verifying the mass graves. With his authorization, checkpoints would hopefully be better. But better than they'd been with Vitaly? That remained to be seen.

It took only a couple of hours before we hit our first major checkpoint and got the chance to see whose influence was better. The road was closed to all civilian traffic at night and hosted a typical-looking roadblock with a bunch of concrete blocks placed to slow our approach to a crawl. There were the typical twitchy guards, but these guys looked even more nervous than usual.

"We're going to be stuck here all night," I muttered as we crawled ahead.

"Just wait," Seaspray whispered as the guard approached.

Seaspray ran through the usual routine, cheerfully handing over our passports and explaining that we were medical guys heading to the front line. But it wasn't until he showed the permit with Chief Vadim's name on it that things changed. Instantly the red carpet was rolled out, and we were waved through with smiles and high praises.

We drove along empty roads for the next several hours, with only Max behind us. Finally around 3:00 a.m., when we were not far from Izyum, we reached a junction and had to make a decision: either carry on heading south toward Vadim to verify the mass graves or pause and stage for an attempt to recover the Marine. There hadn't been any updates on his location for hours, and I was afraid the opportunity might have passed. But we didn't want to move forward until we knew for sure.

We decided to wait a while and get some sleep. Even though it was only September, it was a cold night and raining pretty hard. Max decided to sleep in the warm, dry cab of the box truck, but with our Land Cruiser filled to the brim, Seaspray and I set up our waterproof bivy tents in the tall grass beside the road and climbed inside for the few hours before sunrise.

Three hours later I woke up to a strange sound: a little army of tiny feet accompanied by a constant murmur of quacking. I unzipped my bivy and poked my head out to see a hundred or so ducks making their way through our hasty campsite, followed by an old man with a small staff.

I made eye contact with the duck herder, waved, and greeted him.

"Good morning."

"American?" he replied.

"Yes."

He cursed Putin, gave a deep belly laugh, and followed on after his ducks as they waddled into a nearby field.

I then heard and saw the traffic on the road and I guessed some nearby checkpoint had opened up at daylight. As Seaspray and I packed up in the rain, I could just about hear Max laughing at us from the dry cab of the box truck, with us looking like two homeless vagrants sleeping on the side of the road.

While I'd been asleep Seaspray had received an update about the Marine. The reports were mixed, with some suggesting that he might not be in Izyum after all, while others stated that he was no longer alive. It was a major blow, and it put the search-and-rescue mission on pause. Even so, the mass graves were close, and they still needed verifying. We decided to remain on standby, ready to respond if anything changed with the Marine, but proceeded to the location Vadim had given us—two hours east of Izyum in the red zone: the tip of the spear where Ukrainian troops were pushing back Russian forces.

Driving through Izyum was gut-wrenching, much like Kharkiv. I saw residential apartment complexes, shopping centers, schools, churches, and entire neighborhoods that had been decimated. Just like before, these attacks were in no way collateral damage. They were deliberate, clearly designed to destroy whole communities. They were a tactic that aimed to break the morale of the people and force surrender. I expected to see all this, but it bothered me just as it had at the start of the war. No matter how many times you see the damage that a Goliath-sized enemy can inflict upon a weaker opponent, it still shocks you.

When we finally arrived at our destination, we met Vadim for the first time. Like me, he's a shorter, barrel-chested, middle-aged guy. Unlike me his uniform was perfectly pressed and worn with pride. He was clearly a man who demanded respect, and it was obvious he earned it by the way the men responded to him. I'm sure the fact that he was on the front lines and not back in Kyiv went a long way.

After some initial greetings, Vadim told us it was time to go. But not to the mass graves. First he wanted to take us to the local police station. "We captured some Russians today," he announced. "I want to show you them."

We went first to a building close by. It was brick and single story, with a high fence all around. There was a body of a young Russian soldier just outside the main gate. Vadim looked at me as we walked past it, shaking his head slightly. "Not him. He was dead when we got here. Killed when we regained the town. Come inside. That is what I want to show you."

Seaspray and I followed him. The place was heavily fortified with military fighting positions built onto the corners and blocking the entrances. It looked nothing like a normal police station in America.

"The Russians did all this," Vadim said, waving a hand at the blocked-out windows. "They used this place as their prison. Come."

We walked farther back and down into the basement of the station. There was no electricity, so we lit the way with our cell phones, eventually arriving at a series of eight-by-eight-foot cells, likely designed for single prisoners. People had scratched marks on the walls, counting off the days, weeks, and months. The floors were pooled with blood, urine, and feces. The smell was rancid.

"They kept maybe twenty people in these cells," said Vadim. "Civilians. If they found a soldier, they'd just shoot them."

Farther into the basement we found a room where the walls and ceiling were lined with paper egg cartons, like a makeshift recording studio.

"Deadens the noise," said Seaspray. "Makes it harder to hear what's happening in here."

Vadim nodded. He pointed to a chair in the center of the room.

"They tortured people here. And back there"—he nodded to a doorway that led to a long, low-ceilinged room—"is where they executed people. There are bullet holes in the wall."

I looked in from the doorway. I could see hundreds of empty bullet casings on the floor.

"Now," said Vadim, "I want to show you the soldiers we found."

We followed him back outside and took a short drive to a different site where a single soldier guarded a steel door. Inside were fifteen men who immediately stood up when they saw Vadim enter. They were Russian soldiers, both young and old, scrawny, pale, and tired. They looked like they hadn't seen a bed in months. They didn't say anything, but every one of them looked terrified.

With their eyes locked on Vadim, they stood at military attention. They knew he had all the power as to whether they lived or died—the same power they had held over the Ukrainians they'd captured and held in the police station basement.

"We found most of them earlier today," said Vadim. "Putin issued an order that anyone in his military who loses a telephone or radio will be killed, so most Russian troops have no devices on them to help them know where they are. They get lost easily, especially when they are in retreat. So we found them walking in the woods, and they surrendered. We arrested them and brought them here, in spite of what they did."

Then he pointed to the corner to a man with a hood tied over his head, ankles bound, and hands tied behind his back. "Except for him. He tried to fight us. Let's go."

As we were walking out, one of the Russians started to speak, but Vadim either couldn't understand him or didn't want to listen to what he was saying. He continued walking and led us out.

"Now I will take you to where we found them."

At first we were driving along a straight, wide residential road. In peacetime it would have been a great place to raise a family, especially as within a few miles we were driving into a beautiful pine forest.

First I saw the tanks. There were twenty or thirty of them, some destroyed, many intact but abandoned. All had the white *Z* painted on them, indicating they were Russian. A few tanks had the bodies of Russian soldiers either hanging from doorways or scattered on the ground nearby. Their flesh was swollen and white—they hadn't been dead more than a few days.

We stopped and surveyed the area. It had clearly been the home of a Russian tank unit, and some tanks were still dug in. There were underground bunkers protected by logs and a network of trenches linking each position. They had really fortified themselves to be there for the long haul.

We drove a little farther beyond the Russian tanks to what in many ways looked like a construction site. Trees had been chopped down, making way for tracks in the bare earth where vehicles could drive. There didn't seem to be much order to the tracks, other than the fact that they all led to a clearing where earth was banked up taller than a man's head surrounding large, dug-out pits.

We parked near one of the pits and followed Vadim as he walked slowly toward it. A few soldiers were gathered around—some working, some staring into space and taking a moment. Hardly anyone was speaking.

Someone had put hazard tape around the edge of the earth mound that surrounded the pit, but I didn't need tape to tell me it was a crime scene. I could smell it in the air: the stench of decomposing bodies.

I wanted to take a moment before walking in there, but no matter how much anger or sorrow I wanted to feel, I had a job to do. I needed to focus, to observe what the Russians had done and report back. We needed to bear witness to what we were seeing.

The earth mounds were mass graves. As I watched the Ukrainian soldiers were working through each one: pulling out the bodies, transferring them to a waiting open grave, then burying them in individual graves that they were digging nearby. None of the bodies could be identified, but each was buried with a cross bearing the name of one of the missing people from the town.

The Ukrainians had been working on the site for six days. In the mass grave I was standing by, they had found 475 bodies.

In another grave they had found 1,100 bodies.

Most had been burned, likely to try to hide the evidence. Many had their hands tied in front or behind, a clear sign they had been executed.

They were all civilians. All of them.

Children. Women. Elderly.

It was a war crime. An atrocity. An act of evil.

And from everything I'd seen and heard, this wasn't the only mass grave in Ukraine, and it wasn't a rogue act by an individual commander going behind the backs of his superior officers. What had happened here—the invasion of a town, the six-month occupation that ended when the civilian women and children were rounded up with their hands bound and brought here to be executed—this was a pattern. This was a strategy. This was a logical final step for an invading force that had targeted civilians from day one.

I assured Vadim I would tell the right people about what we witnessed, but it didn't feel like enough to simply file my report back with the intelligence agencies who'd commissioned us in the first place. I wanted to bear witness to the rest of the world, so I recorded a video and sent it to Fox News, who broke the story.

Later, while we were driving away, one of their reporters called. I put her on speaker so that Seaspray could be a part of the interview. When she was almost done, she said she had two final questions for us.

"Why are you guys out there helping these people?"

My answer was equally as simple. "Because it's the right thing to do."

Her final question was directed to Seaspray. His answer will stick with me for the rest of my life.

"Is it worth it?"

"It doesn't have to be," said Seaspray, not skipping a beat.

Those five words summarize everything about our time in Ukraine. It doesn't have to be worth it to do the right thing. Sometimes we just do the right thing simply because it's just that—the right thing to do. There doesn't always need to be an ROI, and we don't have to calculate what we will get in return if we choose to expend our time, money, energy, or resources. We don't need to worry about who gets the reward or who deserves the credit. Forget about whether it's safe, popular, or dangerous. When it comes to helping people in need, the world needs fewer people who are calculating what they're going to get out of it and a whole lot more people who will simply do the right thing.

———

The next day we had arranged to meet up again with Vadim at a location farther east along the front line. As we drove through territory that had only recently been liberated from the Russians, we navigated through minefields, unexploded ordnance, and the familiar sight of blown-out roads. There were dozens of smoldering tanks that had been destroyed by javelin missiles, and plenty of Russian soldiers around—most of them dead, a few still dying. The presence of wet blood and the lack of swelling or rigor mortis told us that they had been killed within the last twenty-four hours. The Ukrainians who had wiped them out were still standing around, smoking and laughing and experiencing that strange blend of calm and relief that soldiers experience after contact. Some were dragging Russian bodies into piles. I was surprised to see Ukrainian medics providing what looked like decent care to wounded Russian soldiers. I made eye contact with one who was missing his arm as a medic was wrapping it. He didn't even look like he was in pain—just relieved to not be fighting anymore.

Beyond the bodies and burned-out tanks was a mix of beautiful pine forests and picturesque fields full of overgrown sunflowers. It was past harvest time, but nobody had been able to get out and work.

The skies were heavy and gray, it was pouring rain, and there was mud everywhere. It felt like a ripe environment for war, and the farther we went, the clearer it became that those same Russian forces who had ravaged the land were still active in the area. All the military checkpoints were on high alert, and every person we encountered looked like they were expecting to fight at any moment. We even reached a point where our GPS stopped working entirely, showing instead the message, "Restricted Area—No data beyond this point." We guessed the Russians must have blocked it, and we had to go old school for a time using a map and compass.

We were in constant contact with the TOC back in Kyiv, as well as Rysko, Vadim, and other people we trusted to give us the latest on the threats in the area. They gave us helpful insights, but the truth of the matter was Russians were all around us.

I checked in with Hunter, who had just finished with Safari and was now taking his team to Bakhmut—a city that, since the invasion in February, hadn't gone more than forty seconds without receiving indirect fire from rockets or artillery. All the same, I still had a sense of peace about him going. I was trusting God.

We were not far from Vadim, crossing a river on a temporary bridge, when the sky above erupted with the sound of incoming aircraft. The noise was unmistakable.

Seaspray continued driving, but we both strained in our seats to see whether it was what we thought it was. A couple of seconds later we had visual confirmation. It was exactly what we both thought: a pair of Russian MIG fighter jets, screaming over the top of us at treetop level.

We were the only vehicle on the road and were completely exposed. The nearest cover was a tree line a mile or so away, so there was nothing we could do but keep driving and hope the MIGs weren't interested in a lone Land Cruiser.

The jets were heading right for the tree line. As soon as they reached it, plumes of smoke rose above the trees.

"You ever seen that before?" I asked, feeling the first waves of relief.

"MIGs flying overhead? Never."

"Me neither."

There wasn't much else to say. And there really wasn't anything else to do other than keep on driving toward our destination, along with hoping and praying that we remained well and truly off the MIGs' radar.

———————

We got to Vadim's location a little later than we expected and were relieved to see that he was already there. Instead of police, this time he was with a unit of Ukrainian soldiers. Every one of them looked exhausted.

I stayed in the vehicle while Seaspray went to talk with Vadim and the troops' commanding officer. After everything we'd experienced in the previous twenty-four hours, it was good to pause and rest up, if only for a moment.

I'd just closed my eyes when one of the soldiers started tapping on the window.

"*Parol*," he said as I rolled down the window, pointing first to his phone then to the roof of the vehicle. "*Parol?*"

I'd picked up a few Ukrainian words so far on my travels, but this one was new to me.

"*Parol!*" he said again, this time holding out his phone for me to look at. He was trying to connect to our Wi-Fi and I figured that *parol* meant password. I tapped it in for him and watched as he stepped away, out of sight of his CO, and hunched over his phone.

I watched him closely as he scrolled. His face was full of emotion. Soon it hit me that this might be the first time in six months that he'd been able to get online and check his messages. The first time in half a year of making contact with his wife, his kids, his parents. The moment where he was able to tell people he was alive. A time to find out who at home was dead.

Soon others came up and asked for the password too. I was happy to share it and to fire up the espresso machine in the back too. It was a privilege to be able to offer something as simple as free Wi-Fi and a cup of hot coffee and see the impact on these guys' lives.

We'd been there an hour or so when Seaspray took the call telling us the effort to rescue the Marine had hit a dead end. After a couple of days with no updates, I wasn't surprised that they'd lost comms altogether. But I was troubled by it, and Seaspray was too. We'd been a long shot, but still a shot. I doubted the Marine would have many more chances at rescue, if he was even still alive.

Then we heard the familiar whistle of incoming Russian artillery, round after round shaking the ground. Seaspray and I took cover as each explosion crept closer to our location. The Ukrainians had it under control and I felt calm. At least, I did until the moment I phoned Hunter and heard the explosions going on around him too.

"We're taking indirect fire, too, Dad. Don't worry. I'm driving like a bat out of hell! We're good. I'll call you when we're clear."

Hunter disconnected before I had a chance to respond.

All this time that I'd spent in Ukraine, meeting those Christians who had sacrificed everything and not lost their faith, and I was still tempted to try and force God's hand. I still wanted to say the kind of prayer that forced God to bend to my will and bring my son home safe.

I guessed that somewhere back home, the parents of the US Marine who was wounded and captured might be praying that exact same thing.

And the people in Izyum—surely they had prayed too?

It didn't take long for our Ukrainian friends to suppress the Russians enough for us to move out in the convoy behind Vadim. Shortly after leaving, Hunter called back and let me know that he had been able to get himself and his guys to safety. But in that time I did a lot of thinking. My thoughts weren't new, not to me, and not to most people. But they were important.

I was thinking about why bad things happen to good people. I was wondering why God would allow those people back in Izyum to be murdered like that. Why would He not stop it? I've faced these same questions many times in my life after being exposed to atrocities to the innocent in places like Afghanistan. Through the years I've been through cycles of reconciling my questions and then bringing them back to God all over again.

As my mind wandered, I thought about Jesus.

If the question is *Why do bad things happen to good people?* the answer has to start with Jesus. He was the only truly good, sinless, perfect person who has ever walked this earth, and He was falsely accused, arrested, beaten, tortured, spit on, mocked, ridiculed, and murdered. He was the best version of what a good person can be, and yet He suffered the worst fate possible. He was God's Son, but even He wasn't exempt from the evils of the world. If that level of suffering can happen to Jesus, then why not us?

To earthly eyes the sight of Jesus hanging on that cross must have seemed like the worst day in history, but to eternal eyes it was actually the best day till the end of time.

God certainly loves us, but He doesn't hand out free passes on suffering in this life. The Bible is filled, cover to cover, with stories of good people who faced tremendous hardship and suffering. But it also tells how God redeemed those hardships for good and for His glory.

It may not be easy to see at times, but I think there's comfort to be found in that. We have to look past the earthly things we face and see things eternally as God sees them. When we can do that, our perspectives will change and we will learn to truly trust God so that He can use us in the way He intended.

War, suffering, atrocities, and other evils are not the last word or the final act. Pain and even death are not permanent. Bad things do happen to good people, that's true. But it's not the end of the story. Not even close.

When we truly grasp that, only then can we learn to trust Him, to listen to Him, to take action in the things He burdens our hearts for. God invites us all on His journey, and while it's not always a pretty one, the reward is eternal. And sometimes accepting that we're on God's journey means that we have to accept that our kids are too.

ELEVEN

THE YEAR I STARTED
LEARNING

The very first time I said goodbye to Hunter before I headed off on my first deployment to Afghanistan, he was eight years old. I stood by my gear, tears rolling down my cheeks, and watched as Kathy drove off from the parking lot. I remember Hunter staring at me through the window, tears on his face, our eyes locked until Kathy turned the corner. I wondered if I'd see any of my family again, and I wondered what their lives would be like without me—either for the months I'd be gone or the rest of their lives if I didn't make it back.

On subsequent deployments it got easier and easier for me to say goodbye, but it always hurt, and Hunter always struggled more than the others. Before my last deployment, when he was eleven, I remember him begging me not to go, crying so hard his little legs collapsed and he was too weak to even stand. I let him sleep with me all night before I headed out the next morning.

With all those goodbyes, I never imagined that there would be a day when I would be the one staying at home, watching Hunter disappear off to fight the same war. But in 2019 that's exactly what happened.

The day Hunter left for Germany and then Georgia to prepare for his deployment to Afghanistan, he came over to the house to say goodbye. He'd been in the Marine Corps for three years already, and apart from a blip right at the start when he enlisted—when I'd had a vivid nightmare about him being killed—I'd been mostly okay with the idea of Hunter as a Marine. It was a great fit for him, something he had wanted to do his whole life, and now he was pumped about finally getting to deploy to Afghanistan. So when he came to say goodbye, I handled it well. I told him all the reasons why I loved him, and all the reasons I was proud of him, and said goodbye.

It didn't take long for me to find out that I was a long way from okay. I was not a normal military parent. I knew too much. I had been to Afghanistan eight times, buried friends there, seen horrific atrocities, and returned home a mess. Since 2011 I had been leading Mighty Oaks and seen so many warriors who were battling with the horrors from their time in Afghanistan. Those who lost friends, became amputees, had TBI (traumatic brain injuries), PTSD, or just lost themselves based on things they experienced. Fear crept into my heart and mind over what might happen to Hunter.

As soon as he landed at Bagram Air Base my anxiety started to surface. The Marines Hunter was relieving got hit by a VBIED (Vehicle-Borne Improvised Explosive Device), killing three Marines and wounding others. Hunter and his teammates were part of the cleanup, so things weren't off to a good start. Old memories of my own deployments came back to me, tormenting me as I worried about my son. My mind was flooded with images of Hunter out on patrol and getting caught by an IED. I would close my eyes and see and hear and feel exactly what it was like to be caught up in kinetic combat. I'd picture him driving in a convoy of his fellow Marines, then imagine an enemy combatant approach and detonate their explosives, turning the air into a cloud of dust and shrapnel. I'd visualize my son's lifeless, mangled body and feel overwhelmed that I couldn't protect him.

Hunter, meanwhile, was loving it. He'd send us messages about things that were going on in the unit, asking us to pray for him when he was going out on patrol. He'd tell us about all the things he was learning, all the experiences he was having. His sergeant major and a first sergeant who I knew well were giving me glowing reports, even calling one time to tell me how he had shot and disabled another VBIED heading into their convoy. Hunter was clearly in the place where he was meant to be and was thriving in combat. Meanwhile, back at home, I was feeling like I was losing the battle completely.

At the time, Mighty Oaks was already well established and thriving. We'd started working internationally and had already built a solid reputation. We were literally saving lives, restoring families, and changing legacies for eternity—hundreds of thousands of people have been helped by Mighty Oaks. Given all that, you'd expect that as founder and CEO I'd have insight into what to do with all the anxiety raging inside me when Hunter deployed. You'd think I'd know how to respond, maybe reaching out to people and putting into practice principles that we were teaching to thousands every year. You'd think that I'd have known what to do, but you'd be wrong.

Instead of opening up, I shut down.

I didn't say anything to anyone.

I tried to convince myself that this was all natural. I figured that I'd work my way through it. I told myself that all parents were supposed to be stressed out when their kids deployed to a combat zone. When I was at my best, I'd get down on my knees and beg God over and over to bring my son back home safely. But as Hunter's deployment continued, the stress and anxiety started to overwhelm me.

It all reached a peak the night I got in my truck. All day my heart had been racing and my thoughts raging. I'd felt powerless and out of control—two states of mind I have never much appreciated. So I'd hoped that a couple of hours unplugging on the jiu-jitsu mats would help. That's always been one place where I can be present in the moment and not think about things that are worrying me.

I didn't even make it to the academy. On the way there I stopped at a grocery store for some supplies, and as I walked up and down the aisles, staring blankly at the products, I could feel the beginnings of a full-blown panic attack.

I started feeling dizzy and knew I needed to sit down. I saw one of those blood pressure machines at the back of the store. I sat down, followed the instructions on screen, and hit the Start button.

After a while of sitting and waiting for the machine to deliver my results, a pair of numbers finally flashed up on the screen. They were high. Crazy high. So I called my buddy, a BJJ teammate who happens to be a heart surgeon.

"Hey, Jose," I said, trying to keep my voice level and calm. "I'm not feeling too good right now. My blood pressure is around 180 over 110. Should I be worried?"

"Those are your numbers?"

"Yeah. I'm at one of those machines in the store."

Jose paused for a second. "Chad, you should probably go to the emergency room."

I drove the mile to the ER, though I have no memory of it. But I do remember the number on the hospital machines: 200 over 130. And I remember the speed with which the nurses and doctors worked to calm me down, setting up an IV, sticking electrodes all over my chest, checking in on me constantly and giving me a cocktail of medication.

The drugs worked that day, but over the next three months I continued to have panic attacks, usually multiple times each day. I took time off work and had to learn how to lean on good friends for support. I reminded myself of the very things we teach at Mighty Oaks.

Two men that mean the world to me—Dr. Bill Peters, a Force Recon Platoon Commander and Silver Star recipient from Vietnam, and Pastor David Baird, who served on the Mighty Oaks board and was an incredible mentor—flew in to spend time with me. I read books. I studied the Bible. I put my trust in the exact same methods we teach at Mighty Oaks.

It took almost a whole year, but gradually I started to understand that through it all God was revealing powerful truths to me:

That God loves the people I hold closest more than I could ever love them.

That God can protect the people I hold closest better than I could ever protect them.

That my job as husband and father is to freely relinquish my loved ones into His hands when situations are not within my control.

By the time Hunter was ready to come home at the end of his tour, I had finally recovered and was in a good place.

———— • ————

Fast-forward five years to April 2023, and I'm standing in my kitchen at home. I'm getting ready to say goodbye to my son before he flies to Ukraine for a mission—a mission that I won't be joining him on. And I'm nervous. My heart is already starting to race, my mind facing that familiar threat to spiral down into anxiety. I can feel the fear scratching at the door. *Hey, Chad. Remember me?* I have to take a deep breath and force myself to calm down. It's all too familiar.

But it's also different.

Hunter is about to lead another mission to Ukraine, but it's not him that I'm worried about. If 2022 has taught me anything, it's that my firstborn son is one of the most reliable, dependable, resourceful men I have ever had the privilege of working alongside. Since the start of the war Hunter has made nine trips to Ukraine, most of them without me. He's spent time with units like Safari, traveling throughout the country, delivering lifesaving IFAKs, training troops in TCCC and how to be spiritually resilient. His comms network now covers almost the entire country, and he has received so many reports of how his work has saved lives. He's calm under pressure and has the most amazing ability to connect with people the world over. When Hunter talks, people listen. And when Hunter listens, people open up. I trust him to do well, and I trust God for him too.

So, no, this whisper of fear that I'm feeling is not about Hunter.

It's about Hayden, my second and youngest son. He's joining Hunter on the trip. He's never been to Ukraine before.

Hayden is a Marine, just like Hunter, just like me, and just like my father. He's smart, clearheaded, and has been working with us at Mighty Oaks for the past year. He and Hunter are going to Ukraine alone, just the two of them, to meet with Ukrainian officials and continue the work with our network of chaplains. But right now, in this moment before Hayden comes over and I say goodbye, knowing all that doesn't seem to be making a whole lot of difference to what I am feeling inside.

I guess some lessons take a while before we really learn them. Or maybe it's just that if we want life's biggest lessons to really take root, we must be prepared to practice them over and over. If we want to grow, we have to be prepared to work.

All the time I was in Ukraine with Hunter it seemed to me like I was in some kind of spiritual exercise. It was as if God had me doing countless reps of the same questions that had been raised for me back in 2019:

Do I understand that He loves Hunter more than I ever could?

Do I believe that He can protect Hunter better than I ever could?

Am I willing to trust God so much that I am prepared to place Hunter in His hands?

It took all those trips out to Ukraine, with all those moments where I could feel the weight of the risks that Hunter was facing, but eventually the learning took root.

And when that happened, the change was one of the best I've ever experienced in my whole life. As I was able to let go of the anxiety of what might happen to Hunter or now Hayden, I started to truly appreciate the ways in which my sons were stepping into the work God had ordained for them. As I took my focus off my own dark fears, I was able to see the beauty of God's providence, to look upon my sons with more pride and gratitude than ever. The more I learned to truly trust God for my sons and relinquish them into the hands of Jesus, the more I was able to appreciate God's love for all my family, and even myself.

In other words, letting go of my fear changed so much more than how I felt about those I love and want to protect. It started to change my faith too—the more I practiced trusting God with my children, the more I wanted to trust Him with other parts of my life.

That's what I need to remember.

I believe that was God's lesson for me all along.

And I think maybe other parents need to know it too.

It's so tempting to want to be in control of protecting our kids, spouses, and loved ones. But we don't have anything like the level of control we think we do. Cars crash, natural disasters hit, cancers grow, and the geopolitical landscape shifts, leaving innocent civilians to face the full force of a First World superpower. We're kidding ourselves if we think we have the kind of strength that can keep any of that at bay.

But God *is* in control. He's in control of all our lives, from the first breath to the last, though the way He exercises control doesn't look the way we might expect. We reach for control out of fear, closing down the horizons ahead of our loved ones because we're just too scared of losing them.

God does it differently. For Him, being in control means being there for us, no matter what we're facing. His arms are always open wide, always inviting us to turn to Him. To rely on Him. To find that in His love, we will find all that we need.

Hayden arrives. He's not looking nervous, but he's looking serious. He knows the weight of what's coming. He knows what he's getting into, what he's risking. And he knows why he's doing it.

"You okay?" I ask when we're done hugging.

He nods.

"On this trip, Hunter's not your brother. He's your boss, and you're in good hands."

Another nod.

"And he knows what he's doing. So do what he says, right?"

"I will. I will, Dad. I love you."

"I love you, too, and am proud of you."

I have so much more to say but decide this is enough. Hayden needs to know that I trust him. He needs to know that I've got faith in him. But more than anything, he needs to know that he has a Father in heaven who loves him one hundred times more than I ever could and he needs to see me demonstrate my trust in Him.

So Hunter, Hayden, and I all pray together.

Then we hug again. I tell them I love them.

And then I say goodbye.

MY DAD AND ME

by Hunter Robichaux

J ust before Dad called me from Izyum to tell me that he was in the middle of some kinetic fighting, I was driving into Bakhmut. I had my three Mighty Oaks colleagues with me, as well as the two Ukrainians, Vitaly and Dimas. The town was empty. Like a graveyard.

We stopped when we saw the smoldering ruins of the bridge in the center of the city. We'd been planning to cross it, but it had been blown out hours before we arrived. It was a good thing too—it alerted us that the Russians were still in the area.

I didn't like where we were positioned. The bridge was overlooked by low hills, and it was totally exposed. I'm an ANGLICO Marine by trade, which means that putting bombs on targets is my bread and butter. I knew we were sitting on a targeted location for artillery or rockets. It left me feeling very uneasy.

It didn't take long before the first shell dropped. It was two hundred meters from our position. At first I thought it would be only one round and that we'd be okay where we were, but the second impact came quickly and was close enough for me to feel the earth beneath my feet shake. Ten seconds later another round hit, this time within one hundred meters. The Russians were creeping rounds our way, and it was time to move and get off that bridge site. Like my dad always says, it was time to "get off the X."

Throughout my work in Ukraine one of the key themes has been taking calculated risks. When I'd first arrived as the FedEx guy, the risk was stepping up and trusting that I could work alongside guys with decades of tier-one special operations experience. Then there were the checkpoints and the risk of getting shot by some nervous civilian-turned-soldier-overnight with little to no training. But standing on the bridge in Bakhmut when the shells came in, I faced what felt like my biggest risk of the whole war—the risk of having to step up to lead when others' lives depended on the decision I made in that moment.

Vitaly and Dimas were still laughing after the first explosion. As a forward observer I knew that all the Russians had to do was make one more adjustment to their previous impact and we'd all be taken out.

"We're going now!" I called out. "Get back in the vehicle."

For a moment Vitaly and Dimas looked at me the way Vitaly looked at my dad when we rerouted out of Mykolaiv.

I stared at them both. When I spoke again my voice was calm, but strong. "Now! We're going now."

They did what I asked.

As soon as my team got into our truck we said a quick prayer together, making a direct call to God to protect us and get us out safely. Never before or since have I ever felt the peace and protection of God more than I did on that rugged street of Bakhmut with bombs landing just one hundred meters away.

Even though it happened more than a year ago—and there's been just as much danger since then—I still think back to that bridge. When I do, sometimes I wonder what would have happened if we'd stayed. What if I'd kept quiet? What if I hadn't decided to drive like I'd been taught in our training package? Maybe we'd be dead. Maybe not.

But most of the time, when I think about the bridge and the bombs, I end up thinking about God. I think about the fact that He had seen that moment coming for years. And more than that, He had led me right there. Being on that bridge was precisely where I was supposed to be at that time.

———◆———

When I was six years old, I had a dream. I didn't know which country I was in, but I knew it was overseas. My six-year-old brain recognized the dusty streets, the men wearing their long and flowing robes, the women in their black veils. But I wasn't there alone. My dad was with me, and in my dream, I knew that meant everything was going to be okay. We were doing some kind of work that I didn't fully understand, but I did know that wherever we were and whatever we were doing, we were helping rescue people who needed it. I liked being there with my dad, working side by side like that.

Suddenly there was chaos and we were running, heading toward a bunch of people who needed our help. Bad men were shooting at us and trying to stop us from rescuing the people. We were in the fight of our lives and had no weapons to defend ourselves, but we still continued to rescue anyone that we could.

The dream ended soon after, and the thing is, my dream wasn't a nightmare. I didn't even feel much fear knowing that those bad guys had the intention of killing my dad and me. All along, I just felt like I was okay. I was where I was meant to be—helping people who couldn't help themselves, standing up to evil.

That dream never left me. It was in my head when I enlisted in the United States Marine Corps, and I thought about it often when I was deployed to Afghanistan too. But even though there were plenty of times when I could help people when I was a Marine, it never felt like the fulfillment of my dream. I always had the sense that at some point in my future, I'd be doing exactly what I'd dreamed about when I was six—helping rescue people with my dad while bad guys tried to stop us.

When the summer of 2021 came round and Dad told the family that he was going to try and bring Aziz and his wife and children out of Afghanistan, I thought about the dream a lot. I figured that this was going to be the moment when it would be fulfilled. Finally I'd get my chance to join Dad in the mission to save lives, right there on the ground, on the dusty streets of Afghanistan with men in robes and women in burkas. I was convinced that it all fit together perfectly.

Not being able to go into Afghanistan personally that summer hurt. I've never been the guy who gets held back, especially as a Marine. I've always volunteered, always wanted to be the first guy to put up his hand no matter what the mission. But in that summer of 2021, when I was told to stay right where I was in Abu Dhabi, I was deeply frustrated. I also understood the position my dad was in as both a leader and a father. I'm sure it wasn't easy for him to make those calls.

I felt the same seven months later when my dad, Seaspray, and the rest of the team rolled out to go rescue Ben Hall. Being told that you're needed more back at the HQ compared to the field is bad enough, but when you feel like it's in direct opposition to something God's got in store for you, it's even harder to accept. Yet God's timing turned out to be perfect in the end.

When God puts a burden on your heart, it's like a seed. It can take a long time before you see any signs of life up above the surface, and even longer until it starts to bloom. But if you water it with faith, if you put your trust in God, that seed will grow. It might not look how you thought it would or sprout when you want it to, but when He is ready it'll grow. And eventually it'll produce fruit in the perfect season of life.

All that is needed is patience. The truth is, I'm not particularly good at patience, but I've had a lot of practice over the last few years. I've found that it helps when I read about other people in the Bible who had to wait a long time for those seeds that God planted to bear fruit. People like Abraham, Joseph, Moses, David, and even Jesus Himself. There's a ton of waiting around in the Bible, and people who find themselves learning patience, even the hard way, often get closer to God in the end.

It took twenty years for me to begin to feel like my dream was finally about to be fulfilled. It started the day I was driving into Ukraine, my dad at my side. That was a moment that I'll never forget. After all those years of waiting, that first sign of fulfillment was even more special. I'd never really doubted God's love and faithfulness to me, but it gave me the best example I could hope for of how God holds the whole of our lives in His hands. He doesn't let us down and He doesn't walk away.

I've learned so much from the work in Ukraine.

Like the fact that God can—and probably will—call you to either do something that you don't feel like you're qualified for or something that you never really thought you'd be involved in. That can lead to self-doubt, as we start to wonder whether we're good enough, accomplished enough, or equipped enough. But remember this old truth: God doesn't call the qualified. God qualifies the called. That's been so important to me this last year.

Then there's the fact that God often trains you along the way. He uses situations and circumstances that are outside your usual experience. So while being surrounded by chaos, death, and destruction is sad and disturbing, it's also a great opportunity to learn more about God, about yourself, and about the calling He has on your life.

And the things you learn in the middle of those extreme situations—those are some of the most precious and powerful life lessons of all. All the adversity I've encountered in Ukraine has only served to deepen my faith. It means that I am even more determined to put Christ at the center of everything I do personally and professionally. Every time I've come home from Ukraine, I realize how much I take for granted and I'm grateful all over again that my family lives in peace.

I've learned that working with your father isn't always the easiest thing in the world, but I am grateful to my dad for bringing me with him and, more important, for letting go in the balance of loving me, protecting me, and trusting me. As a father myself now, I know that one day I will face the same challenge of letting go and trusting God with my own children's safety and future. I'll have learned how through watching my father navigate the transitions of parenting from fear to faith.

EPILOGUE

If you remember only one thing from this book, remember this: It can take years for the things that God places on your heart to start to flourish, but when they finally do, it's not the end of the story. It's just the beginning.

CONCLUSION

Since the Russian invasion of Ukraine on February 24, 2022, I've made ten trips there. Hunter has made fifteen, and Mighty Oaks team members have together made over thirty trips to support the people of Ukraine in their fight for their lives and freedom.

Our work during the remainder of 2022 involved embedding teams from Mighty Oaks within the Ukrainian military to provide soldiers with medical supplies and TCCC medical training. These efforts were not surface level; our teams forged deep bonds with the soldiers, living and engaging with them during combat and everyday life. This closeness allowed us to share the message of hope and faith with these brave men and offer lessons and resources from Mighty Oaks spiritual resiliency programs.

As we transitioned into 2023, we concluded our work with Safari Group and other units. The networking and relationships established the previous year allowed us to move into the next chapter, the work we believe God brought Mighty Oaks to Ukraine to do. Since 2011 Mighty Oaks has not only provided spiritual resiliency and recovery programs for over half a million warriors in America but also trained pastors all over the US to care for the military and first responders in their communities. Recognizing the crucial role of volunteer chaplains in Ukraine—predominantly pastors and ministers desiring to support citizens and soldiers from their communities—we wanted to support and equip them.

We were positioned to help in a profound way. Through relationships with the Ukrainian government, local military units, churches, and nonprofits, we began training camps to turn pastors into military chaplains. These chaplains were equipped to serve on the front lines and in the trenches with the troops, bringing hope, encouragement, and the Word of God while possessing the basic skills to survive in a combat environment without being a liability to those they were serving.

CONCLUSION

As of April 2024, Mighty Oaks has trained and certified over three hundred chaplains. Looking ahead, we're planning a program to enhance their spiritual resilience, ensuring the continuity of our mission long after our departure. Our vision for Mighty Oaks International extends beyond Ukraine. We're empowering chaplains to independently conduct spiritual resiliency and recovery training under our banner, fostering self-sufficiency and sustainability in future efforts. Saving lives, restoring families, and changing legacies for eternity: a true mission without borders.

ACKNOWLEDGMENTS

One of the greatest honors of my life has been traveling around the world with my team and going into war zones to help the most vulnerable. Many of our operations are not publicized or put into books like this one. However, when we do talk about them, there is often lots of praise and credit given for the work. But the real heroes are often behind the scenes—those who provide invaluable support that allows us to be focused on the missions at hand. Our spouses keep our homes in order, our children safe, and our spirits high. Our staff at Mighty Oaks carries the extra load of running daily operations in our absence so we can continue serving our military and first-responder communities. And thousands of people around the world support our efforts financially, through many words of encouragement, and by interceding in prayer.

Finally, I'm grateful for everyone who helped bring this book to life. As you can imagine, it is no small task to put together a book like *A Mission Without Borders*. I'm especially grateful to my writing partner, Craig Borlase; my agent and dear friend, John Howard; the amazing team at Thomas Nelson; and the incredible humans who have lived the stories captured in the pages of this book. I am blessed to be surrounded every day by some of the best people this world has to offer.

ABOUT THE AUTHOR

Chad is a former Force Recon Marine and DoD contractor with eight deployments to Afghanistan as part of a Joint Special Operations Command (JSOC) Task Force. In 2011 he founded Mighty Oaks, which has touched the lives of more than half a million individuals within the military and first-responder communities through faith-based resiliency and recovery programs.

In 2021 Chad led a rescue mission into Afghanistan, which saved over seventeen thousand lives, including his Afghan teammate, Aziz, and Aziz's family. The story is chronicled in his bestselling book *Saving Aziz*, which is set for a cinematic adaptation.

Chad is a retired professional MMA fighter and world champion, with a fourth-degree black belt in Brazilian jiu-jitsu and an MBA from New York Institute of Technology. He and his wife, Kathy, have been married for twenty-nine years and have two sons, two daughters, and four grandchildren. As a board-certified pastoral counselor and subject-matter expert on PTSD and veteran care, Chad's insights have influenced policy at the highest levels of government, including presidents, senators, and congressional members. Through his podcast—*Resilient*, media presence, and public speaking, Chad has inspired millions worldwide with his message of hope and resilience.

MIGHTY OAKS
★★★★

Mighty Oaks is committed to serving military and first responder communities who have endured hardship around the globe through intensive, peer-based discipleship programs, outpost meetings, and speaking and resiliency events. There are programs for men, women, and married couples at multiple locations nationwide and globally. Those who attend our programs are fully sponsored— including meals, lodging, and travel—ensuring their sole focus is on recovery and empowering them to identify their purpose as they move forward.

⊛ **RESILIENCY**
⊛ **RECOVERY**

GLOBAL OUTREACH ⊛
ADVOCACY ⊛

"To restore the brokenhearted through Christ, to build leaders of leaders to rise up from the ashes; they will be called Mighty Oaks of Righteousness." — Isaiah 61

MightyOaksPrograms.org

APPLY HERE

SCAN TO DONATE

RESILIENT

Resilient, a podcast hosted by former Force Recon Marine Chad Robichaux and former SWAT officer Sean Kennard, is a show dedicated to empowering individuals and strengthening society through the cultivation of true resilience. In a world filled with confusion, self-doubt, and emotional turbulence, it's time to reclaim our strength and adaptability.

We believe that true resilience extends beyond physical prowess; it encompasses a robust integration of the mind, body, social, and spiritual pillars.

2024 guests include Terry Crews, Shawn Ryan, Lyoto Machida, and more.

LEARN MORE

LIVE RESILIENT.COM

A MISSION WITHOUT BORDERS
PHOTO GALLERY

MISSIONWITHOUTBORDERSBOOK.COM

Printed in the USA
CPSIA information can be obtained
at www.ICGtesting.com
LVHW031245111124
796283LV00017B/823